PEEKING THROUGH THE KEYHOLE

# PEEKING THROUGH

# THE KEYHOLE

## The Evolution of North American Homes

AVI FRIEDMAN & DAVID KRAWITZ

McGill-Queen's University Press

Montreal & Kingston / London / Ithaca

© McGill-Queen's University Press, 2002
ISBN 0-7735-2439-8

Legal deposit third quarter 2002
Bibliothèque nationale du Québec

Printed in Canada on acid-free paper

McGill-Queen's University Press acknowledges the support of the Canada Council for the Arts for our publishing program. We also acknowledge the financial support of the Government of Canada through the Book Publishing Industry Development Program (BPIDP) for our publishing activities.

**National Library of Canada Cataloguing in Publication Data**

Friedman, Avi. 1952–
Peeking through the keyhole : the evolution of North American homes / Avi Friedman and David Krawitz.

Includes bibliographical references and index.
ISBN 0-7735-2439-8

1. Housing–North America. 2. Architecture, Domestic–North America–History.
3. Architecture, Domestic–Social aspects–North America I. Krawitz, David. II. Title.

NA7203.F75 2002        728'.097        C2002-901806-4

This book was designed and typeset by David LeBlanc in Adobe Garamond 11.3/16.5 in Montreal, Quebec

*To our parents who gave us our first homes*

*Haim and Dina Friedman*

*Gerald and Estelle Krawitz*

# Contents

# Preface

Homes, whether in wood, stone and brick, or in concrete and glass, have always been a physical manifestation of the culture, values, and economic status of the people who inhabit them. Home in North America can be a house in the suburbs, a downtown apartment, a cottage in the country, a single room at the end of the hall, a duplex, a houseboat, a mansion in the hills. Whether we care to acknowledge it or not, the home we live in proclaims our social standing and reflects the trends of the times.

Not surprisingly, trends in housing are subject to history and fashion. They come and go and return again, to the delight of some and the torment of others. In the latter half of the twentieth century and at the beginning of the twenty-first, trends have become truly ephemeral: some last only a season, a month, or they may seem to complete their fragile life cycles in a single week. Whether it is the width of a tie or the curve in the hood of a car, the urge to buy a particular colour of paint or the decision to dine out on one cuisine instead of another, trends are in fact highly complex, each one the product of some perceived notion of collective taste, marketing strategies, and mischievous raids on behavioural patterns of the past. Trends in homes – in both their outward appearance and the use of the spaces within – are no less subject to the vicissitudes of period and culture. But houses are meant to last decades and centuries, not seasons. The trends that determine their design and purpose fall and rise according to cycles somewhat more extended than those governing a popular tune or software application.

Until the past few decades, transitions in the style of homes and in the types of households who inhabited them were slow and gradual. Builders constructed houses according to the dictates of standard conventions: proportions, sizes, materials, colours were all subject to accepted norms which varied little from year to year. Universal, instantaneous communication and transmission of visual images have changed the way we observe the dwellings and lives of other people. Television and the Internet have let us into the homes of the entire world, revealing households in countries we will never visit, showing us our neighbours in their kitchens, living rooms, and bedrooms. We witness local trends and global trends with equal ease. No matter where a style or certain look or even a simple detail comes from – we see it and we want it. We rush out to have it made real in our own lives.

Quite apart from our electronic forays into other homes from the comfort of our armchairs and desks, the past few decades have transformed our lives at home at a remarkable pace and in ways that would have been formerly unimaginable. Infants are placed in daycare so both parents can go to work. Single men and women buy homes with no intention of sharing them with any other person. Electronic equipment to facilitate our work and play requires space in rooms which now have not only new functions but new names: media centres, entertainment rooms, home offices. Couples have fewer children than their parents and need to lodge them till a later age. While some householders crave ever larger homes to satisfy their longing for more toilets and sinks, taller ceilings, and a third garage door, others surprise themselves by moving into compact spaces which they would have never imagined when they were younger.

Yet in North American society we all still live in rooms with walls that have doors and windows, we prepare our food in kitchens, we sleep in bedrooms, and wash in bathrooms. Some of our most basic human activities are not subject to trends or to socio-demographic shifts and economic restructuring, and the changes in our homes, while radical, still follow an evolutionary logic. The novelty of our age is that the evolutionary process is an accelerated one. Our use of the spaces in our homes changes with a rapidity that can be confusing and disorienting. And as we transform these spaces, they in turn transform us.

This book is about the transformations that most North Americans have undergone since the middle of the twentieth century. We have marked the end of the Second World War as the starting point for our observations. The late 1940s and then the 1950s were the time of the mass popularization of the automobile and the rise of suburbia, the growth of the modern homebuilding industry, and the emergence of social and cultural phenomena as diverse as consumerism, reliable birth control, and television.

The motive for the book was the recognition that the events of recent years have altered the process of home design, which must now acknowledge and incorporate a host of factors that are not directly related to the design process. The recent changes in our homes have touched all households and they present themselves in every corner of the house, apartment, condo, mobile home or room we live in. These transformations are the result of demographic, economic, lifestyle, environmental, and technological pressures. Some have left only a superficial imprint on our homes and have a marginal influence on the domestic environment; others, such as the effect of consumption on home buying, have a far more significant impact.

Homes cannot be detached from the activities that take place inside them or from the material culture that influences their content. For this reason, we have discussed not only the spaces and materials in homes but the people who live in them and the objects that surround them. We have observed how the world around us has changed our lives and our households, and how many of our homes have not kept pace. For a surprising number of people, the types of homes available out there do not match their needs. Many would-be homeowners have been priced out of the market, many cannot find homes that suit the way they live, and many have simply been left by the wayside in their pursuit of one of the most basic components of the North American Dream.

We wanted to peek through the keyholes of our homes and see what was going on inside. We looked at how we feed ourselves and communicate with one another, how children are raised and people age, and how we build and choose our homes. We decided not to limit our view to the house and its occupants, so we ventured out-doors as well, to discover how homes fit into the larger context of a community and how they have become commodities at the centre of sophisticated marketing strategies.

Standing on the threshold of the twenty-first century, we cannot make the clock stand still nor can we undo the changes that continue to sweep us along, but we can offer a fresh way of looking at the home. We wanted to offer a sense of reason and sanity to the dilemma faced by us all at one time or another: how do we carve out a piece of home that we can call our own?

# Acknowledgments

The catalyst for the writing of this book is the changes that homes have undergone in recent decades. Demography, lifestyle, and technology are among the issues that have left their imprint on home life. Social changes have been foremost in our field of vision.

Our teaching, research, and writing on housing in the past decade at the McGill School of Architecture have provided a suitable foundation for our observations. We are grateful to the director, David Covo, and to our colleagues for the friendly and supportive environment that has made our work possible.

We thank Michelle Chan and Barbara Vokac for so carefully and diligently digging up necessary statistics and background data.

We are grateful to our editor, Diane Mew, and to the staff at McGill-Queen's University Press – Joan McGilvray, Susanne McAdam, and Margaret Levey – who were so helpful and friendly, and in particular to Philip Cercone, who was always encouraging and who supplied constructive guidance.

Finally, we thank our families for their patience and support.

PEEKING THROUGH THE KEYHOLE

# Introduction:
# The Accelerated Present

W hen the first members of the generation born after the Second World War turned fifty in 1996, North America was bombarded with stories on the baby boomers. The first great outpouring of attention paid to the boomers had already occurred in the late 1980s, with articles and books devoted to the suddenly vital issue of demographics. For a business to succeed or a new product to take off, we were told, the boomers had to be the prime target market. A backlash of disgruntled murmuring was inevitable, the young protesting that the boomers had grabbed all the good jobs, the elderly claiming that the attitudes and lifestyles of their children had overwhelmed television, movies, and advertising. People of all ages pointed to the hypocrisy of the boomers, saying they had sold out the generous liberalism of the 1960s in anticipation of a conservative and acquisitive middle age. Whatever the opinion may be, the simple fact remains that a specific chunk of the population, born in an eighteen-year period following the Second World War (from 1946 to 1964), makes up almost one-third of all people in the United States and Canada.

In the coming decades, as the boomers get older and raise the median age by five years, we will notice greater numbers of old people in society and fewer young people. The change will be gradual, but the ratio has shifted in the past few decades and the effects will become increasingly apparent. The generation which follows the boomers, the baby bust (born 1965 to 1976), will outnumber the boomers only by the year 2040, and the boomers' children, the baby boomlet or the boom echo (born 1977 to 1994), will outnumber their parents in 2020. All those people in their late thirties, forties, and mid-fifties – the greying children and teens of the 1960s – form the largest age group and will continue to dominate in numbers for decades to come.

Whether we like it or not, the boomers' needs will affect the needs of us all. The drive to provide homes for them as they move through their various life stages towards old age and death will prompt designers and builders to create homes that suit the type and size of boomers' households – first as parents, then as empty-nesters – their lifestyles, and their tastes. The modification of the current housing stock and construction of new homes will leave behind a housing legacy that will affect how all North Americans live for many years to come.

Domestic life has changed so significantly in the years following the end of the Second World War that it would be useful to examine some of the transformations in our households and families and in the jobs and lifestyles of people of all ages. The better we understand these trends and changes, the clearer will be our picture of their effect on current and future directions in housing. The household seems a reasonable place to begin.

There are well over a hundred and ten million households in the United States and Canada, with over a million new ones added every year. But while the number of households increases, the average size of each household is shrinking and its composition is changing. Since 1940 the average number of people living in a home has shrunk by one person, to just over two and a half. Almost three in five households are made up of only one or two persons. Large households are simply not that common: homes with five or more people account for only one-tenth of the total. Families are just not as large as they used to be. Many adults grew up in families with three or four brothers and sisters, but when it came time for these adults to have their own kids, they have produced only two, on average. It should come as no surprise that while large homes are still being built, many buyers are searching for smaller, cheaper dwelling units more suited to their scaled-down requirements for space.

Most of us would assume that the majority of households are families and that most of these families are made up of mom, dad, and the kids. No shock here: these assumptions are still true. As recently as 1970, four out of five households were families and the other one was classified as non-family. Today that proportion has shifted: two family to one non-family. But the traditional family is losing ground. Whether with children or without, married couples occupy just over a half of all homes, a marked decrease from three-quarters of all households in the early 1960s. Married couples *with* children, on the other hand, make up less than one-quarter of all households, a significant drop from almost a half in 1960. Other households considered families include male-female couples who are not married or single parents. That still leaves the growing category of non-family. Such a household could be two friends living together, a group of people sharing a house, or the increasing number of households of men or women who live with non-relatives, including gay and lesbian couples. The growing market for housing types perceived as ill-suited to traditional families — highrise condos, rowhouses, duplexes – is supported by rising numbers of households who are themselves considered non-traditional.

The vast majority of non-family householders are people who live on their own. Single dwellers have tripled their share of total households since the war: one in four of all homes now belongs to a lone occupant. Certainly, many homes are filled with single people who have lost their spouses or are between marriages and relationships, but most people who live on their own are not marking time. Their dwellings are permanent homes for people who need space for only one. And for many of these householders, a two-storey house or even a bungalow would not be as reasonable as a 500-square-foot downtown condominium.

Men and women used to marry young. For those over forty, this phenomenon is a living memory, but for younger folk, the discovery of this quaint fact often comes from watching a movie in black and white or flipping through *Life* magazine or finding the parents' wedding album and realizing, with amazement, what kids those folks were when they tied the knot. Although people still marry in their early twenties, the overall tendency is towards a later marriage. In the 1960s only one woman in ten was not married by the time she turned thirty; now one in three remains unwed at the end of her twenties. Not surprisingly, childbirth has also been delayed. Most women still bear their first child in their twenties but increasingly women are waiting until their thirties. Access to reliable forms of contraception, greater numbers of women pursuing and establishing careers, and evolving perceptions of traditional roles for both women and men are all factors. What used to raise eyebrows and set tongues wagging – a woman marrying and having her first child after the age of thirty – is now so commonplace as to be barely a topic of conversation. The upshot of later marriages is a greater proportion of people living longer as singles – as individual men and women who might buy homes as singles and who will defer their purchase of a family home till later than their parents.

Single parenthood is not a recent development in human history, as many who bemoan the decline of traditional families assume. Advances in medical science and workplace safety have reduced the numbers of widowed parents in our society; the very term "young widow" is far more rare than it used to be. And there have been and always will be women whose impregnators have abandoned them and their own children. Two fairly modern developments have contributed to the sharp rise in single parenthood: divorce and personal choice. "Personal choice" is perhaps a vague way of expressing any number of situations in which a woman decides to become a parent alone: the decision of a single woman to carry through with an unexpected pregnancy and not to have an abortion or give the child up for adoption, the desire to proceed with parenthood unencumbered by a husband or live-in mate, or the decision to have a child when no suitable male life partner is in the picture. Whatever the cause, more than one-quarter of all children under eighteen live with only one parent, more than double the 1970 rate. Four out of ten children do not live with their biological fathers. Single parents and their children certainly live in any and all of the housing types favoured by two-parent families. But with a host of competing needs and schedules – not to mention restricted budgets – it is understandable that many single parents do not live in some of the more traditional versions of "family homes."

Marriage is, if not exactly endangered, at least a troubled institution. Two-fifths of all marriages involve at least one person who has been married before. As a result of divorce, many children live with only one parent, or one natural parent and another "new" parent, or alternating combinations of natural parents and their new partners. Three out of ten children now live with a divorced parent or with parents who never got married, whereas in 1960 it was one in ten. One in twenty babies was born to unmarried parents in 1960; today the rate is almost one in three. The result is a redefinition of the family, with the possibility of additional households, new parents and grandparents, in-laws and siblings. Children can still have only two natural parents, but their potential domestic arrangements have become challenging and complex.

Children today begin their pre-school life earlier and in greater numbers than their parents did. One simple explanation is that almost seven in ten mothers work for pay. For the first time ever, families in which both parents work are in the majority even among married couples with children. One result is that almost a quarter of all pre-school children are in child care. The term "child care" as we know it has a markedly different meaning from what a mother in the 1950s and 1960s would have supposed: it refers not simply to the time and energy devoted to the child in the home, but to the organized supervision of children by hired staff who are not the parents of their charges. Following child care, or preceding the beginning of formal schooling in kindergarten at the age of five, children increasingly attend various forms of pre-school: just over a third of all children went to pre-school in 1970, but more than a half now attend. Formerly known as nursery school, the new education for youngsters aged three and four results in a home that sits empty for much of the day. Such a home benefits from a design which matches function and space differently from a house with a stay-at-home parent. And a home where parents and children interact for only four or five hours a day operates more efficiently when outfitted to perform as an ally of busy and frequently stressed householders.

The process of growing up for children involves a growing away from their parents: from a crib in the next room, to a room down the hall, to a space in the basement (if they're lucky and if such a place in the home exists), and finally to a home of their own. In recent years this process has slowed down. Jobs are getting harder for young people to find. Rents in many cities have risen steeply, so that children stay in their parents' homes longer than they used to. The milestones of life achieved with such apparent ease by their parents – finishing school, getting a job, making their own home – are further from the grasp of young people today. Over one-fifth of all twenty-five-year-olds still live with one or both parents. Living at home longer has become a necessity, a new fact of life.

Before moving from the realm of families and households to the subject of the economy and our lifestyles, we should pause and reflect on whether or not the portrait sketched so far of the North American household seems at all improbable or unrealistic. If, for instance, you are currently married, have three children, and the wife stays at home looking after the kids while the husband goes out to work, if you were married young and have never been separated or divorced, and all the people you know have similar lives, with no younger children in day-care or children in their mid-twenties living at home, then perhaps our statistical picture appears far-fetched. If, on the other hand, you have been married more than once, or you have never been married and you live alone or with parents, and you have only one or two children or siblings or none at all, or you are a single parent, or you live on weekdays with one parent and on weekends with the other, then you are aware that what we are outlining here is not a fabrication. Our aim is to point out that the familiar concepts of home and family are in a state of evolution which forces us to reconsider the way we house ourselves.

When it comes to matters relating to the economy and society, most people could be excused for believing that the middle class just isn't what it used to be. In fact, one might have the impression that the wealthy are getting richer and the poor poorer. Viewed from the centre, the middle class certainly appears to be shrinking, or at least redefining itself. If we examine the idea of middle class as a function of household income, and choose an annual range of $25,000 to $50,000 or, more broadly, $15,000 to $75,000, in both cases the number of earners in these categories has been going down. More people have been "leaving" the middle class and joining the ranks above or beneath them than those who have become members of the middle class by dropping from above or rising from below. Stagnant wages are the most probable cause; real wages adjusted for inflation rose steadily every year throughout the later 1950s and the 1960s but crept forward at a miserable rate from 1971 onwards. A body of middle earners with shifting status will have a marked effect on the housing market. Builders and designers who make certain assumptions about the budgets of their prospective clients are revising their products as well as their expectations in line with changing demographics.

Government budgeting for deficit and debt reduction in recent years has led to cutbacks in social services and jobs. Much of the social spending of the immediate postwar decades has been reconsidered or cancelled in recent years as governments reorient their priorities and dismantle many of the programs now deemed wasteful or inefficient. Aside from direct government spending, recessions and sluggish growth between boom periods tend to weaken the confidence of investors, employers, and everyday consumers. During good times people often spend lavishly and even imprudently, but the merest hint of a downturn is enough to spread feelings of unease and pessimism. Home building and ownership reached record levels just before the turn of the millennium; not long afterwards, nervous consumers clutched their pocketbooks tightly at the first signs of a burst bubble.

Many North Americans have been affected directly by the restructuring of traditional arenas of commerce, which has resulted in redundancies and unemployment for those who once considered they were in secure lifelong positions. The economy has been moving steadily away from industrial production in favour of services and information processing and analysis. We have also heard much of corporate downsizing and its effect on both high- and low-paying jobs. In the early 1980s half of men aged forty-five to fifty-four could claim that they had been with the same employer for thirteen years, but by the late 1990s this figure had shrunk to ten years. The majority of the executives of large corporations expect to use more temporary help in the coming years. Contract work saves money for employers but does little for the ability of employees to plan their futures. Security is the key word here. Without the prospect of a job that can be depended upon, earners are hesitant to undertake long-term financial obligations such as mortgages. Housing developers find they build more low-ticket homes than they used to, not for a specifically low-income clientele but for wary buyers who are reluctant to commit themselves to large monthly payments when their next career change might be right around the corner.

In the face of such prospects, it is encouraging to fall back on the optimism of youth. When polled, almost all teenagers believe that they will have good-paying jobs as adults, while three-fifths of teens believe that they may be rich some day. No sooner had the media dispensed with Generation X than they came up with Generation Y, the youngest group now reaching adulthood, the so-called Ritalin generation. Whereas the X-ers came of age during bleak times (bad job prospects and mounting national debt), the Y bunch grew up during years of solid economic growth. Those born in the early 1980s have high expectations for good homes and jobs. It remains to be seen whether their hopes will be fulfilled or dashed.

At the opposite end of the age spectrum are those over sixty-five who still work: one in eight, the highest proportion in over two decades. Many would-be retirees are reassessing their ability to stop working now that companies have cut pensions and medical coverage and governments have banned forced retirements and made changes to social security. The phenomenon of people working later in life will have an effect not only on home use and resale but on the perception of home as a vital part of one's portfolio as much as a place to flop into bed.

North Americans can be big spenders, but they also manage to save some money, too. The rate of saving of after-tax income has been dropping, though, over the past few years. For those who track such figures, one can find monthly spending rates which exceed income and which can be explained by our society's casual dependence on credit. Death and taxes: perhaps *debt* and taxes would be more to the point. Seven in ten people have at least one credit card, and two-thirds of credit-card holders carry a balance from month to month. The average amount of that debt per user household is over $2,000. When it comes to taxes, two-income families spend almost two-fifths of their income on taxes (up from one-quarter in 1955), which may seem an inevitable fact of life, but which is twice as much as they spend on homes and households. Two obvious questions present themselves. If families where both spouses work spend twice as much on taxes as they do on their home expenses, is the cause of home-ownership properly served? And if the majority of credit-card holders maintain a perpetual balance, paying interest every month, does such spending run counter to taking on a major expense like homeowner-ship, or does it contribute to a healthy overall economy by keeping money circulating? We leave these questions open to debate because we certainly do not pretend to be able to answer them definitively.

Lifestyle changes are more difficult to quantify than social and economic fluctuations. Numbers of children born, hours per day worked, and median ages are all knowable facts that can be assigned numerical values. Attitudes and habits are intangible concepts, further from the statistician's clipboard or keyboard. For our present purposes, we can consult polls and surveys to arrive at some examples of past and present behaviour in the home – for instance, the amount of housework performed by women.

It may come as no surprise to learn that women in the paid workforce spend less time doing housework than full-time homemakers, and that the average time spent on housework by all women (two and a half hours per day) is far less than the time spent in 1965 (five and a half hours). Of concern to us are the implications: the changes to spaces in the home and to the function of particular rooms when certain traditional activities are scaled down. In other words, we have recast the placement of objects in the home (for example, washing machines) now that some household tasks are combined in an effort at time-saving multi-tasking. Some householders (particularly those without basements) find that baking a cake and doing the laundry at the same time are made easier by placing the washing machine either in the kitchen or directly adjacent to it. Chores involving water (cooking and washing) have been located for centuries in the same area of the home – the rear – but it was a novelty for many dwellers of the late twentieth century to discover that kitchen and laundry facilities have been deliberately located in the same room. Designers of homes have had to rethink counter space, appliance placement, and circulation in the kitchen area to accommodate old functions linked as new neighbours.

When people make claims about the amount of stress or happiness in their lives, it is impossible to say to what extent such assertions are fair assessments of their own emotional states or highly subjective impressions based on feelings and fallible memories. Nevertheless, almost a half of all people claim that they have less free time than they had five years earlier, a third say they always feel rushed, and over a half report feeling stress at some point in the preceding two weeks. Regardless of how these claims are measured and verified, when people say they could use more leisure time and less stress, we can take for granted that they are definitely experiencing a degree of strain, that they are testifying to an overly busy lifestyle. With two of out five people working over sixty hours a week, and the same proportion reporting that they are so tired they have trouble staying awake at work, we can safely assume that a great number of people are run ragged. Stress, overwork, and sleeplessness fall within the professional domains of therapists and employers, but they are also topics that have an impact on use of the home. The demands placed on a home are different for a person who works nine to five and has the time and temperament for plenty of gardening or an array of hobbies from the needs of a person who gets home late in the evening and spends a concentrated amount of time in one particular place (the living room, for instance), undertaking a limited range of activities (falling asleep on the couch in front of the TV).

Many people work hard to provide themselves with the basics of life but they also work hard for their toys and holidays. The average annual spending on sports, audio-visual items, pets, toys, and hobbies is about $2,000 – about the same that is spent on clothing or on vacations. Material possessions and activities which would have been deemed luxuries in earlier decades are now commonplace in many households; they are objects and experiences reasonably considered to be within the realm of achievable expectations. But they are part and parcel of a lifestyle of hard work and hard play, of pressing schedules which leave people drained whether they are earning or spending. They also point to a new attitude to budgeting shared by many of today's earners. Rather than devote all their savings and wages to a single huge expenditure, purchasing the most expensive home they can afford, they commit to a lower-priced home and smaller mortgage, leaving some cash for restaurants and trips, electronics and toys.

Computers and the Internet are recent additions to our lives and homes, and they have an undeniable impact on our use of time and allocation of space. Over half of North Americans have access to the Internet, and the number of users increases year by year. The average age of Internet users is rising, while their average educational level and socio-economic status is falling, a sign that more people of all kinds are using computers for online activities. Computers at home are used for work and for games, for banking, purchasing goods and services, and for pure entertainment. Activities that used to be relegated exclusively to the office and retail sectors have been shifted to the home, and certain activities that used to take up time and space at home have been dumped in favour of computers. Builders of homes have responded with the installation of wiring and connections to facilitate online and electronic use, while designers have assigned new functions to old spaces (computers in the living room, for instance) and have planned for new spaces to accommodate new uses (home offices and media rooms).

When we finally step back to consider a life of labour and acquisition and its rewards, we are forced to wonder about home base, about the ultimate point of return and how well it serves us on a day-to-day basis. Do new possessions require more space? Or have we revised our conception of the rooms in a home and converted old spaces to new uses? If we have less free time to enjoy our homes, do we require less space? Or have we simply rearranged the traditional outline of rooms and functions?

These questions and the trends we have profiled give some sense of the issues we will treat in the coming chapters. Let us now turn our full attention to homes. We will start where most days begin and end: in the kitchen.

# What We Eat, Where We Eat

For the average middle-aged shopper born and raised in North America, a visit to a massive suburban supermarket would not cause anything like the shock that would be experienced by, say, a person used to buying food at outdoor stalls in China, or even an older person, born in Cleveland or Toronto, who has managed to spend her life inside the suburban belt, picking up her groceries at a neighbourhood store with three aisles and two check-out counters. Our younger shopper, accustomed to supermarkets and shopping malls that have expanded in size over the years, is unfazed by megastores and hypermarkets with a hundred thousand square feet of floor space. But imagine the disorientation of the foreign shopper used to piles of produce on tables and live fowl in cages, or the elderly shopper from a small North American town.

Take the two of them for a drive beyond the heart of the metropolis to the expressway zone, to the land of the long left-turn lane, and show them the superstore off in the distance, across the vast parking lot, beyond the expanse of concrete and glinting metal and glass.

Accompany them into the store itself and observe their reaction to the scene before them. Let your eyes adjust to the strange pinky-orange light, at once bright and uniform, not harsh or blinding yet evocative of no particular type of light found in nature, and try to see what your visitors see.

The space inside the hypermarket is enormous, way beyond the scale of a store where people shop for orange juice or ketchup. The store is so big that a small village of sub-shops is laid out inside the entrance: counter islands where shoppers can buy eyeglasses, drop off their films and pick up photographs, browse through music cassettes and CDs, have a heel replaced on a shoe. Beyond the line of fifteen or twenty check-outs the walls are covered by huge cardboard cartons stacked to the ceiling, boxes filled not with food but with appliances such as refrigerators, washing machines, clothes dryers, and dish-washers. The aisles are formed by very tall shelves and freezer units, all of them stuffed with products packaged to within an inch of their lives: two-pound cartons of breakfast cereal shrink-wrapped together in groups of three, a dozen large jars of mustard available as a single unit (enough for a ballpark of hot dogs), and heavy boxes of breaded and deep-fried chicken wings, frozen and ready for the microwave. You might think this was a showcase for plastic wrap and glossy coated cardboard. But no, there is food inside these containers, and the shoppers pushing carts as large as compact cars are moving with great purpose to buy enough food to see themselves through the next month. This is not panic shopping. The quantities might seem to indicate a desperate provisioning against a coming disaster, stocking up to fill cellars and garages with emergency rations. The shoppers are not anxious, however. Their mission is to save money by buying in large amounts, and they are doing their best to fill those huge carts.

Not all people shop at monster foodmarts. (Not all people have cars. Neither do they all have large freezers and plenty of storage space.) Many still do their food shopping at a number of time-honoured locations: at the corner grocery store which may still deliver; at the twenty- or thirty-year-old supermarket, found in smaller centres or in cities downtown, the humble cousin in terms of size to the suburban warehouse emporium; at outdoor markets which nowadays are preserved as much for local colour as for neighbourhood convenience; and on the way home along a major urban street, stopping in at the butcher, the baker, the organic juice-maker. But the existence of the suburban hypermarket and the increasing numbers of people who do their shopping at such stores are indications of a new stage in the acquisition and consumption of food. The scale and scope of such huge shopping facilities – their reason for being, in fact – are in keeping with new technologies and changing lifestyles which have affected not only the way we pick up the groceries but the appliances we use in the kitchen and our activities in this most central room of the home.

The composition of the food we eat has changed, some would say for the worse. At the turn of the twentieth century, a typical diet included fruits, vegetables, and non-refined grains. Today, although we receive produce from around the world and in all seasons due to a complex transportation and distribution system unimaginable only fifty years ago, we eat far more refined and processed foods and obtain more calories from fat. Fat is the food with the highest energy for the lowest cost, so it's cheap and filling. Nine out of ten households buy potato chips, on average every three weeks. We drink less milk and more soft drinks than we did only a decade ago – a matter of convenience as well as marketing and advertising. We eat more frozen french fries than fresh potatoes – a sign of our spending less time in the kitchen preparing food and more time heating up frozen foods or catching meals at fast-food restaurants. The freezer in the basement or at the edge of the kitchen is an appliance without which many households simply could not function.

Our consumption of certain food products points to our changed ways in the kitchen. For example, we eat twice as much cheese now as we did twenty years ago. This is not because more people have become vegetarians or lovers of dairy products, but because cheese is such a key ingredient in so many fast foods (like pizza) and frozen foods (like scalloped potatoes or greens mixed with cheese). Whether people actually need vitamin supplements to compensate for inadequate diets or take them to feel better about ignoring nutrition, the number of people who take multi-vitamins is surprisingly high: over half of women in their twenties and early thirties, for instance, and over a third of men the same age. To be sure, many people still eat in a healthy and sensible manner, but only a quarter eat three square meals a day without any snacking, down from a third ten years ago.

Food is available in ways that did not exist mere decades ago to satisfy ways of living that are also recent and new. Prepackaged salads account for over two billion dollars of supermarket business per year. The new phenomenon of purchasing ready-to-eat, home-cooked-style meals at the food market, convenience store, or gas station and taking them home to eat – known as home-meal replacement – is now a business worth $100 billion annually. The pace of life has changed for many and with it the style and substance of provisioning. With many mothers working outside the home and children attending daycare and other events away from home, people now tend to eat more frequently and at a greater variety of locations. Spending on food accounts for an average of one-seventh of a household's total spending. And for every five dollars spent on food, only three dollars are for food in the home. North Americans eat meals outside their own kitchens with casual regularity, and fast food is a popular choice: adults go to fast-food restaurants an average of six times per month. If the balance in a person's life at work and at home has shifted, then it follows that behaviour in the grocery store, supermarket, restaurant, and kitchen will have been altered as well.

To say that the shape, function, and organization of our kitchens are evolving is nothing new. The basic purpose of the kitchen – the place in the home where food is prepared – has remained the constant which binds together the changes in kitchen location and size throughout the centuries. The kitchen as we know it today is arguably the most important area in the home and as such it is the most frequently renovated. It serves as a nerve centre for the entire household, where people can relax without caring what to do next or where the family can gather to plan activities and make special announcements. The kitchen table can be used to fill out income tax forms as easily as it can be used by children for arts and crafts. It is a desk when it is covered with bills and a cheque-book, a sewing table for mending and hemming clothes, or even a repair shop or assembly line. Since it is a room with many cupboards, it often serves to store household items which have nothing to do with food: shoe polish and rags, brooms and mops, hardware and tools. The kitchen is the hearth, the focal point of the household. If only one light is left on overnight in the home, it is usually in the kitchen.

The kitchen in North America has taken many forms throughout its history to arrive at its current incarnation. Originally, it was part of the largest room in the house – sometimes the only one – the room where the big table and fireplace were located, the place for eating, working, and relaxing informally. In early New England homes of the seventeenth century, the kitchen of one-room houses was sometimes extended into the outdoors by having the fireplace protrude through a wall so that cooking and candle-making could have their own space away from the single indoor room that was also used for living, dining, and sleeping. A two-room home would be divided into the parlour, for formal occasions and guests, and the hall, for everything else (living and dining, sleeping and working, cooking and eating). In French-speaking Acadia in eastern Canada, the word for kitchen was not even used until the end of the eighteenth century, since the common room with the fireplace was used not only for food preparation but for protection from the damp and as a heat source. Finer houses in New England in the eighteenth century – the sort of habitations that had plastered ceilings and panelled or papered walls – had separate kitchen, dining, and living rooms, with the kitchen located at the back of the house. In the southeastern American colonies of the seventeenth century, cooking was done indoors over an open fire in the early days but was later moved to a building apart from the house. Even in the larger homes of wealthier households, kitchens were either in a wing in the rear or separate from the house altogether.

A typical middle-class home in the Midwest in the nineteenth century consisted of a parlour, usually kept closed, bedrooms, and a kitchen which served as the family gathering place and dining room as well as the food preparation area. In England, to use the classic rowhouse as an example for purposes of comparison, the functions of the kitchen right up to the early decades of the twentieth century were divided into wet work (food preparation and laundry), performed in the scullery at the back of the unit, and jobs involving heat (primarily cooking), located in the kitchen which was part of the general living area in front. When cooking and wet work were amalgamated into a single room, combining the kitchen and scullery, the remaining space was divided into a room for daily activities and a parlour, left unheated except when it was used on Sundays and for formal events. In both North America and England, homes with as few as two rooms would assign a formal function to one of the them – the parlour, a room normally used no more than once a week – and a multi-purpose function to the other space which included, of course, the kitchen.

During the nineteenth century the different functions of the house were compartmentalized into separate areas. The public and private rooms were kept apart, and the kitchen was located either in the basement or in a service wing at the back of the house. In the later decades of the nineteenth century and the early decades of the twentieth, the placement and role of the kitchen became the centre of a political debate involving housewives, feminist activists, economists, designers, urban planners and experts in the domestic science movement. Kitchens were built smaller to make them more scientifically efficient. Three major strategies were developed in the arena of domestic reform during the years from 1870 to 1930: Catherine Beecher's haven strategy, to release the housewife from her domestic drudgery through better design; August Bebel's industrial strategy, to move traditional household work into the factory, thereby abolishing the female domestic sphere; and Melusina Fay Pierce's neighbourhood strategy, to socialize housework under women's control through neighbourhood networks.

The first decades of the twentieth century were a time of specialization and industrialization in the kitchen, with a new focus on appliances and time-saving devices. As the function of each space in the home became more distinct, the kitchen came to assume its exclusive role as a food-preparation area. The typical turn-of-the-century bungalow had a compact kitchen, no larger than 120 square feet. There was no room for a dining table but at least everything was well within reach of the cook. Kitchens were proportional in size to the house itself, so that a large home had a correspondingly larger kitchen.

Where do we find the kitchen today? In the contemporary equivalent of the one-room home, the bachelor or studio apartment, the answer is simple: centrally located, set against a single wall, integrated into the living and sleeping area. In anything larger, the kitchen will rarely share its space with any other room. No matter how compact the overall home, the kitchen will be its own room, even if that means the kitchen is no more than a galley, a passageway between counters, cupboards, appliances, and sink. In houses and apartments built before the Second World War, the kitchen is almost always situated in the rear. The older kitchen in the larger home follows a long-standing tradition in its location: apart from the more public realm of the home (the living room, the parlour), also separated from the private space (bedrooms), at the back of the house where, everyone understood, it belonged.

Contemporary kitchens have become larger and have migrated towards the middle of the home. The postwar era beginning in the middle of the twentieth century was marked by an expansion in kitchen size. Even by the early 1950s the minimum size for a kitchen had grown to 150 square feet. With an increase in floor space came a corresponding change in layout, from the tight galley plan of the efficiency kitchen and the step-saving U-shaped layout designed to keep all surfaces and appliances within arm's reach of the homemaker, to the plentiful dimensions of the island kitchen or the central-table lay-out where a wide U-shape surrounds a large table accessible on all sides. Where once a minimal number of steps and movements within a kitchen were deemed to be the prerequisite for an ideal, efficient design, today's ample kitchens appear to encourage longer distances and wide-open spaces.

Our current attitude to the kitchen has brought it to a point in its evolution where it combines the centrality of the one-room home with the room-of-its-own status of the larger home. No longer banished to the rear, central by choice and not by necessity, an eminent room in its own right, large and warm and inviting, the kitchen is the core of the home. Still and always the functional room where food is prepared and cooked, it also a comfortable room and a showcase room, at the same time utilitarian and unashamedly on display. As the control centre for the household, the kitchen must be efficient and accessible, a room with machines as well as a friendly ambience.

Showcase kitchens nowadays are composed of a variety of materials: marble, wood, glass, copper, and steel. Certain features are combined to create effects that seem deliberately disorienting: huge medieval-style hoods over state-of-the-art multi-function ovens; wooden spoons and wire whisks hanging over built-in, integrated appliances. Formal dining rooms have been eliminated in many homes to create large eat-in kitchens, and the family room has been built adjacent to the kitchen to create the so-called great room. Stainless steel appliances with a commercial look are popular, as are counter levels in a variety of heights. Cabinetry with classic detailing, water filtration systems, convection ovens, silent dishwashers, multi-function service islands: wealthy homeowners like them, builders and real estate agents love them, manufacturers and advertisers promote them as absolute musts.

The common features of any kitchen include a surface for preparing food (countertop, tabletop), a source of water and a drain (sink and faucet), a heating device (stove/oven), a cooling device (refrigerator), and storage facilities (cupboards and shelves). Anyone renting an apartment, for instance, would expect to find these components as the minimum requirements in a kitchen. Add the vessels and implements which owners and tenants alike are expected to possess (dishes, pots and pans, cutlery, and various kitchen tools), and the functional kitchen is complete. Of course, such a kitchen would be considered a stripped-down, bare-bones affair by the standards of many. Where, for instance, are the food processor, the dishwasher, and the microwave oven – relatively recent but indispensable appliances? And what about the electric juicer, the toaster oven, the waffle maker, the blender, the electric mixer, the coffee grinder – items which are not just wedding presents but basic tools for working in a kitchen with ease and efficiency? Are they requirements or simply options? Do they make kitchen work lighter and our lives better? Do we really need them?

Many of the kitchen conveniences which we now take for granted have been with us for over a century: hot water, refrigeration, electric ovens, freezers, dishwashers, electric brooms. Some people can still recall ice boxes and cold-water flats, but for the most part our main kitchen appliances are updated versions of devices that were invented and refined late in the nineteenth century or early in the twentieth. Very few people would advocate a return to the older technologies; we take for granted that our humming appliances will do their work for us in the kitchen. Curiously enough, though, these labour-saving devices have not liberated us from housework.

Dolores Hayden, in *Redesigning the American Dream: The Future of*

*Housing, Work, and Family Life*, points out that "household standards have risen but women's time has not been saved." We may have better washing machines than we had back at the turn of the century, but the full-time housewife spends more time doing laundry now than in the 1920s. We own more clothing, we consume more, and we are fussier about the appearance of our clothes. Although our hands may be less red and raw than our grandmothers' thanks to superior machines and detergents, we spend more time than they did doing the wash.

Ruth Schwartz Cowan, in *More Work for Mother: The Ironies of Household Technology from the Open Hearth to the Microwave*, explains how, with the help of advanced technology, the burden of work on women's shoulders has actually increased: "Modern household technology facilitated married women's workforce participation not by freeing women from household labour but by making it possible for women to maintain decent standards in their homes without assistants and without a full-time commitment to housework." Basically, women were able to take up work outside the home because machines allowed them to perform their housework *and* maintain a paying job. Appliances and gadgets allow us to achieve more in a given amount of time, but because we have heaped on ourselves a greater burden of work both inside and outside the home, we don't see any direct payoff from this increased productivity in terms of extra free time. Cowan explains: "The end result is that, although the work is more productive (more services are performed, and more goods are produced, for every hour of work) and less laborious than it used to be, for most housewives it is just as time consuming and just as demanding."

Enter the new generation of labour-saving devices. The first wave – washing machines, fridges, vacuum cleaners – allowed women to keep their homes clean so efficiently that they could venture into the world of work outside the home. The second domestic technology wave – food processors and microwave ovens – has arrived to help householders cope with the new stresses created by a lifestyle of numerous obligations within a condensed time scheme. The housewife of fifty years ago, if she didn't work outside the home, had a full plate nevertheless: cooking, cleaning the house, laundry, caring for the children, organizing family events. Although such a housewife would put in more time with her household duties than the average paid-work week of forty hours, she was still able to provide certain "services" that many mothers who work outside the home simply cannot do, such as cook a full breakfast or prepare a supper with homemade soup and dessert. The contemporary working woman (or man, if it's the father in the family who shares the big domestic chores such as food preparation and house cleaning) is less likely to have the extended blocks of consecutive, available hours needed to make a full, soup-to-nuts dinner every single night or provide freshly baked goods on an ongoing basis. Our time has been broken down into multiple, condensed units, and a kitchen appliance such as the microwave oven lets us make the most of the compressed time we have allotted for kitchen work.

Part of the reason we embrace new technologies and integrate them into our household routines so readily is that we welcome the opportunity to reduce our household and domestic obligations so that we can move on to the relaxation part of the day when we leave work behind and spend time with our children, or even just read or watch television or go out to a movie or whatever it is that we do with our free time (if any such time exists) before dropping into bed. We want efficiency and leisure, productivity and relaxation, work and luxury. We've even developed a new vocabulary to describe our new patterns of work and play, with words and phrases such as multi-tasking and maximizing potential and quality time. Technology has enabled us to work more and do more and also to get more and have more. We simply want *more*.

Whether our new appliances have actually assisted us in our daily hectic schedules is open to question. There can be no doubt that an appliance such as the microwave oven is in fact a brand-new device which performs a function in a manner unknown to previous generations. No regular kitchen oven can bake a potato in seven minutes. No toaster oven can heat up a plate of leftovers in sixty seconds.

Microwave cooking was developed as a byproduct of military research into radar technology. The microwave oven was discovered inadvertently, when a radio technician noticed in 1945 that the microwaves he was working with had melted a chocolate bar in his pocket. The first microwave ovens were made for us Navy submarines, then for airlines, institutions, and the commercial food industry before a compact model designed for domestic use came on the market in 1967. Nine out of ten North American households now own a microwave oven. Most people use them to heat up leftovers and coffee and to prepare processed foods.

The microwave oven is an original, the genuine item, and not a frill or gadget. People nuke their food not because they are being trendy or to flatter themselves that they are being innovative but because they want to cook or heat up their food faster. Everyone is aware of the limitations of the microwave oven – soggy crusts, uneven heating, microwave-unfriendly dishes, exploded eggs – but we can live with them, just as people used to accept the regular defrosting chore which was part and parcel of owning a non-frost-free refrigerator. The question remains, however: do people use a kitchen appliance like the microwave oven as an integral part of their daily routine of food preparation because it merely saves a few minutes here and there, or because it actually makes possible and facilitates a whole new style of shopping and eating? No one could claim that a household would base its whole daily schedule on a single electrical device in the kitchen, but it is surprising the extent to which a family's eating patterns can depend on its existence and use.

Picture a busy, two-income family with children. Home life is focused, in many respects, on the kitchen. The kitchen is the main operations centre of the household, the busiest room in the home. It is not unusual in such households for all week-night dinners to involve the freezer and microwave. Only weekends and holidays provide the opportunity to cook slowly and adventurously, to whip up old family favourites and experiment with new recipes. It would not be preposterous to imagine three out of the five week-night dinners made with food that has been partially processed in advance and frozen: skinless, boned chicken defrosted in the microwave and prepared for the oven or frying pan, or a main course cooked on the preceding weekend, hauled out of the freezer and nuked. Dinner for the other two nights could be main courses purchased from the mega-supermarket, completely prepared and boxed, needing only removal from the freezer, then microwaving: lasagne, fish sticks, chicken nuggets, pizza, quiche. The shopping for these freezer-to-table meals, together with the frozen chicken, salad fixings, desserts, and juice for lunches, can be done once a week, on the weekend, at a large suburban supermarket which shares a parking lot with the hardware depot and the electronics and music emporium where other household necessities are obtained. One park, one stop for all the week's shopping: convenient, time-saving, and economical. Some shopping, of course, is done locally during the week: drycleaning, pharmacy, and video movies at a commercial strip on a main street, and daily perishable groceries from a corner store.

To say that owning and using a microwave oven is the central focus of family life would be to overstate matters, but the whole manner in which many contemporary households shop for food and prepare meals is based on using the microwave for defrosting and rapid heating. A conventional oven could do the same job but it would add from thirty minutes to an hour to the evening kitchen cycle: time which is not available in many homes. If the device did not exist, the day might have to be rearranged to accommodate a different style of provisioning and feeding. Other activities would have to make way for the additional time needed to do kitchen work. The household would run less efficiently.

The convenience provided by frozen food and commercially prepared meals caters to the desire of the majority of homemakers to reduce the time they spend getting dinner on the table. More than half of women claim to spend thirty to sixty minutes preparing the evening meal, but most would prefer to spend less than half an hour making dinner. People who buy convenience foods know that they are paying a premium because someone else, somewhere else, is preparing food for them. They also feel that the time saved is worth the additional cost. Buying food that has been prepared outside the home represents the relocation of cooking away from domestic kitchens to industrial plants. Some convenience foods are fully made and only need to be heated up, some are presented as premade ingredients which must be assembled into a meal by the consumer, and some are premade ingredients which must be put together with other, unprocessed ingredients to form a complete meal. All of these prepared foods come to us from the farm or the shipping container via the processing plant. Whether a box of frozen spinach or a ready-to-eat, restaurant-quality meal purchased at the supermarket, these increasingly popular convenience foods arrive at our tables after having been handled by many more pairs of hands than our own. These are hands that have not only picked, cut, sorted, and packaged our food – common enough treatment for basic foodstuffs such as fruit and vegetables – but have actually made us our dinner.

Frozen foods have been around for over seven decades. Clarence Birdseye developed a quick-freezing technique in 1924 that kept food cells and the texture of food intact. Frozen foods hit the market in 1930 and were advertised as a way of obtaining fruits and vegetables year-round and of ensuring the consistent quality of meats. The first frozen prepared foods appeared in 1939, including roast turkey, chicken dishes, and various hors d'oeuvres. Whole frozen dinners packaged in trays with three compartments were introduced in 1945 to be served to army personnel aboard aircraft and were transferred to the public realm in 1953.

The past twenty years have been a busy time in the frozen-food realm: cook-in-the-box vegetables, single-serve packages, low-calorie entrées, low-price meals, fast-food items for retail distribution, family-size portions, kids' portions, wide selections of appetizers, and more. Not surprisingly, the main consumers of these products are baby boomers who are single or divorced, although the incredible variety of frozen foods indicates that families with children are also major purchasers. Retail sales of all frozen foods in the United States total over twenty billion dollars annually (compared with one billion dollars per year during the 1950s). The freeze/thaw cycle of meal preparation has reduced the art (or chore) of making a meal to a series of simple tasks involving a shopping cart, a visit to the check-out counter, a freezer, a microwave, and the kitchen table. Of course, people still buy basic food ingredients and make meals the old-fashioned way. (By "old-fashioned," we mean chop and dice, steam and broil, fry and bake, not hunt and gather, pluck and winnow, churn and knead.)

A seemingly necessary byproduct of the culture of convenience in the food industry is the massive amount of packaging used to contain and enclose the food we buy. Each North American throws out five hundred pounds of packaging per year, or about ten pounds per week. This amount of trash makes up a significant portion of the total garbage generated from residential sources. Approximately half of food packaging is paper and paperboard, and the other half is metal, plastic, and glass. Consumers pay for all of these boxes, bags, and jars, although they might not appreciate that for every dollar they spend on food, on average nine cents goes towards the packaging. The excessive and wasteful style of presenting food on shelves in the supermarket can be seen most clearly in individual-portion foods, where small quantities of food are wrapped, grouped together with other identical packages, and wrapped again. Examples of this kind of packaging are serving-size containers of yogurt and pudding, individual cheese slices, and miniature packets of everything from coffee to peanuts. Much of the food packaging that consumers regularly throw away can be recycled: aluminum and steel cans, soda bottles, milk jugs, cardboard, paper, and glass. The methods and frequency of collecting recyclable materials vary across the country, from weekly curbside pick-up to drop-off centres to nothing at all. Recommendations about the size of the space needed for sorting recyclables therefore depend on the type of removal program in place, but the space itself should be near or in the kitchen (the source of most waste as well as the place to rinse the containers) and close to other garbage (for throwing out the non-recyclable components and to encourage people to think twice before tossing everything straight into the trash).

We make our own choices about the food that ends up in our shopping baskets at the supermarket, but much of that food has been carefully placed in our path in a sophisticated and sometimes devious manner. More than four cents of every dollar we pay for food goes towards advertising. The food-processing industry sells its products by appealing to our lifestyles, making us believe that each advertised item is exactly what we need. Low-fat snacks and dressings are aimed at those of us trying to reduce the fat intake in our diets, while rich chocolate desserts and premium ice cream are pitched deliberately at those who care little for healthy eating. The milk industry has attempted to increase its market share by expanding the image of the average milk drinker to include glamorous adults in addition to children. Breakfast cereal manufacturers have also been gearing their ads at adults in an effort to promote cereal as a food item that can be eaten by a group other than children and at a time other than breakfast. Originally introduced to the public over a hundred years ago as a health food, breakfast cereal is now sweeter than ever, as much a snack food for any age group at any time of day as a nutritional convenience for kids in the morning.

Food producers and advertisers also strive to tailor the placement of their products in as precise a manner as the tools of the industry allow them to do. Information obtained from the scanners which read product barcodes – analysed in conjunction with geodemographic data and test panel findings on the shopping habits of consumers – allow supermarkets to determine local demand for particular products and product categories. When store management identifies the needs and desires of their own neighbourhood shoppers, they can make fine-tuned adjustments to product inventory, product placement, in-store promotions, and pricing policies targeted at specific groups. All of us would like to think that we make personalized, informed choices when we reach out to select items in a food store. We make our decisions freely and willingly, but numerous forces (both hidden and apparent) guide our hands.

The major changes since the Second World War in the placement and status of the kitchen in the North American home also involve opening it up to other areas of the home. In the past few decades, kitchens have been enlarged and walls have disappeared or been made into partial walls to facilitate the interaction between people in the kitchen and those in adjacent areas. Both men and women, when canvassed for their opinions in surveys, choose models of open kitchens over the older style of enclosed kitchens. But while walls come down and the kitchen migrates from the back of the house to the middle, certain features of older kitchens, also abandoned over the past few decades, are either making a comeback or are reasonable candidates for revival.

James Wentling, in *Designing a Place Called Home: Reordering the Suburbs*, suggests at least four kitchen details which deserve consideration in contemporary design: eating nooks, walk-in pantries, island counters, and accessible rear doors. "Today's breakfast areas lack the charm that the smaller eating nooks offered," Wentling writes. "Nooks were characteristically cramped but cozy spaces, drawing from the intimacy that small spaces evoke. There's a sense of togetherness that results from dining in close quarters. Home builders can still offer eating nooks with built-in seating in production houses on an optional basis." Such nooks, often standard in modest prewar homes and generally tucked into small spaces, fell out of favour because of their "site-built nature and extensive millwork costs." They could easily be reintroduced and built inexpensively (countertop table, plywood benches), even in affordably priced homes, given the will on the part of builders and buyers. Walk-in pantries have begun to reappear in more expensive homes which provide the luxury of additional space next to the kitchen. "The idea of a large walk-in pantry should eliminate the need for some overhead cabinetry," Wentling suggests, "which in turn helps to open up the kitchen to adjacent rooms. With households tending to buy supplies in larger quantities, larger pantries are again gaining favour."

Island counters, already very popular in recent design, recapture the function of work tables in older country kitchens: a centrally-located, multi-functional surface with unimpeded access. They reinforce the role of the kitchen as the focus of the home by allowing people to work together more easily and to interact comfortably while engaged in food preparation. Finally, an accessible rear door (in kitchens located at the back of the house) makes eating outdoors a natural extension of kitchen activity. "While outdoor dining is the main reason for direct kitchen access to the outside," Wentling explains, "it is interesting that most new home designs have access doors to the rear from either the breakfast or family area instead of the kitchen workspace itself. The most direct path for bringing out food would indicate that the door be closer to the central part of the kitchen."

In the design of kitchen spaces, we sometimes overlook features from the past which could enhance the comfort and efficiency of our homes. We would do well to re-examine features which may been heaved overboard in the headlong rush to relocate and demolish, to be innovative and contemporary. An essential aspect of creating good livable spaces for ourselves is to ensure that evolving concepts in design do not discard details and ideas which have not yet outlived their usefulness.

Now that kitchens have become areas of such prime importance in the home, it should come as no surprise that they have also become key selling points for those who market homes – the builders and real estate agents. The layout of the space, the arrangement of the appliances, the amount of light that a sliding door or skylight lets in are all components of a question asked by those searching for a user-friendly home: Can this room be my ally in coordinating the packed schedule that is my life? When a prospective buyer strolls through a kitchen in the company of an agent, and stands at the sink and gazes through the window, or lets a hand trail along a countertop, or inadvertently slides open a drawer, that person is testing a machine, not unlike the browser who slips into the driver's seat in an automobile showroom. The buyers want to know if the colour suits them, if the overall impression reflects their personalities, if this is a kitchen in which they can cook *and* entertain. Will such a room make dinner preparations for an unexpected visitor easier and less stressful? Will this kitchen make me happy and proud? Will it draw compliments and confirm my selection of this home as a wise choice?

Tract builders and real estate agents are aware of their leverage in the marketing of homes and have learned to play to buyers by pushing design-correct kitchens. A large patio door or window can fool a buyer about the size of a given space; natural colours are chosen to give as little offence as possible; and a wide array of displayed gadgetry caters to our urge to have fun and to make our domestic working lives easier. The kitchen is presented as a status symbol and can be quite ostentatious, with accents in marble and wood, glass and gleaming metals. People who fancy themselves as amateur specialists in the kitchen love the hanging pots and pans, the convection oven, the enormous amount of counter space, even if the style is sometimes a strange mix of farmhouse and hi-tech, ranch bungalow and space shuttle. When homeowners count on the inside of their homes to establish a strong sense of identity for themselves, the kitchen can be forced to assume a huge load as the standard bearer for the whole house. No longer is it the room in the house for sale where the agent addresses the wife of the couple and points out to the little lady what a delightful workspace she'll have. The kitchen is now the *pièce de résistance*, the highlight of the tour, the room which must satisfy *all* members of the household.

One of the joys of homeownership is that people with means can make what they will of the spaces they inhabit. Builders can load houses with features they believe will reel in the buyers, while prospective owners can demand that their kitchens look like a page out of a magazine. Whether outlandish elements and stylish touches contribute to resale value or not may be beside the point to many buyers and sellers. The kitchens they create provide instant gratification, no matter that they may be dated in five years or excessive to their needs or even downright silly.

The priority in designing and selecting a kitchen for a home is that it suits the needs of its users, that it makes a match between home and occupant, that it is *right*. The home may be huge or compact, the owner may be prosperous or humble in means, but the kitchen should always be suitable, efficient, flexible. No one can demand that the kitchen *must* be in the middle of the home, that it *must* be open to all other rooms. One can only hope that the product fits the consumer. And when the consumer is given a measure of informed choice and input into the configuration of the ultimate product – the home – the likelihood is that the fit will be snug.

# 2

# Webs and Wires

Fifty years ago the only electric devices which brought information from the outside world into the North American home were the radio and telephone. An after-dinner evening of family entertainment could easily have been an hour or two of radio, the household members sitting on overstuffed chairs and sofas in the living room, all of them listening to the same show. Father would make the selection, and no one dared to object. If he smoked or rustled his newspaper too much, again, no one complained. Mother sat silently and listened, relishing these moments of relaxation, this welcome break between a long day of housework and the final task of putting the children to bed. Depending on the radio show, the children would either join their parents in the living room or play elsewhere in the home. Whether in the living room or hallway or their own bedrooms, they made sure to keep quiet and avoid any disturbance which might interfere with their parents' listening pleasure. The sudden ringing of the telephone would be an interruption, a loud and clangorous event. Heavy, black, shining, perched on its own small table in the front hall, the telephone was a special object in the home. Its ring was a fanfare, an announcement of significant news. The telephone ringing was like a knock on the door: you could not ignore it. You stopped whatever you were doing to find out who it was and what they had to say. If the phone rang in the middle of the evening meal, Mother might say, "I wonder who could be phoning at dinnertime." If it rang during a favourite radio show, Father might be irritated, he might consider the call an intrusion, but he would deal with the matter immediately.

Fast forward fifty years. Today's dad is lying down after dinner in his bedroom, channel surfing. The telephone rings, and he looks over to the display on his bedside phone and sees that it's not for him, so he ignores the call and lets someone else in the house answer. The VCR player attached to the bedroom TV is taping a show that Dad hopes he might watch later with his wife, without commercials, before bedtime. In the meantime, he's flipping with the remote control, hopping around the million-channel satellite universe, catching a bit of local news here, some national news there, five minutes of a sitcom, a segment of a documentary, an exchange or two on a talk show, a music video, even a cartoon. Mom is downstairs in her home office, finishing up a presentation for a meeting the next day, glancing every now and then at the clock on her computer screen, realizing that she won't have forty-five minutes to watch the show her husband is taping. She had promised earlier that she would make some time for them to spend together at the end of the evening, but as she waits for a crucial e-mail message and frets as she tries yet again to access a busy website, she knows that she'll probably be fast asleep before the show's opening credits are over.

The children are also plugged into their own electronic worlds. The daughter is in the living room, enjoying prime time on the large-screen TV and receiving calls and e-mails on her cellphone and messages on her pager. On the weekend her father hogs this prize viewing location, but during the week it's hers. She's watching the key network shows that will keep her up to date with the lives of the doctors and nurses, teen witches and vampire slayers that she follows with such anxiety and interest. Her father bought the enormous entertainment unit for the whole family, but in the end she's the only one on the leather couch in front of the 54-inch screen. The last member of the household, the son, is also in front of a screen. He's up in his bedroom behind a closed door, at his desk, glued to the computer (a hand-me-down from his mom). He claims to be doing homework, and everyone knows he spends a lot of time on chat lines and playing games, but what they don't know is that he's chatting with a woman he's never met hundreds of miles away, pretending that he's twelve years older, the president of his own company, and a keen racketball player. His father is proud that he has such a studious son.

In the immediate years before the Age of TV, the living room was the centre of family life. The few communication devices were centrally located, restricted to particular places in the home, and shared by all members of the household. Five decades later, connections to the media and information sources are to be found in almost every room in most homes. In the years following the Second World War, new spaces were created to accommodate activities unsuited to a formal living room or parlour: the family room, outfitted with a television set and with furniture that could actually be used by children, an informal place where people could relax and spread out; and the rec room, usually in the basement and basically an indoor playground.

Both of these new rooms were created when the baby boomers were children, and their development coincided with the emergence of television as a presence in every American home.

The early boomer years were the time of the first generation of TV, a period followed by families purchasing second television sets for use by kids in spaces devoted exclusively to their activities. The telecommunications era in the 1980s, 1990s, and first years of the twenty-first century has packed the home with electronics: radios, computers, stereos, and televisions distributed throughout the house, miniature movie theatres replacing traditional rooms. To look at the home as a container for communication devices is to find a series of several viewing and listening spaces.

Today's living room is laid out with the contemporary hearth – the television screen – as its focus: sofas and armchairs arranged for optimum sight lines, dimmer switches for controlled lighting evocative of a cinema, entertainment units plugged into satellite and cable TV and the videocassette recorder (VCR) or digital video disk (DVD) player. We have become spectators and auditors rather than people who interact with one another in the home. Instead of gathering together to share a form of entertainment as a household, we run off to our separate spaces to enjoy alone a TV show, a taped movie, a computer game, a dialogue over the Internet with a person we have never met.

The realm of audio in the home is marked by a profusion of devices and a miniaturization of components: we possess many telephones and radios and stereos, players for cassettes and compact discs and music downloaded from the Internet, and they have become increasingly compact. Radio was invented over a century ago, and regular broadcasts have been standard in North America since the 1920s. The single household radio of the prewar period – the size of a small oven and encased in wooden cabinetry – has given way to lightweight instruments in a variety of forms: the bedside clock-radio, some models no larger than a hardcover book; the portable clip-on radio for jogging, as small as a pack of cigarettes; the radio as a component in a stereo system, which together with the amplifier and cassette and CD players might take up no more space than a portable television set; and the lightweight, waterproof, battery-powered radio for use in the shower. People wake up to the radios in their bedrooms, eat breakfast and read the paper while listening to the kitchen radio, drive to work or take the bus without a break in the morning show, and exercise, do housework, or sit in front of the computer wearing headphones. When the only radio in the home was firmly planted in the living room as an independent console or as an element in a gigantic hi-fi (a 1950s marriage of electronics and heavy cabinetry, enclosing record player, amplifier, radio, speaker, and storage place for vinyl phonograph records), and with some lucky households possessing additional radios in the kitchen or master bedroom, the experience of listening to the radio was linked directly to specific locations in the home. Portability was not an option, and the likelihood was high that more than one listener would make up the home audience.

Today two people listening to the radio together is more the exception than the rule. Household members, each person in a different room, can listen to different radios simultaneously, oblivious to the activities of everyone else. The home as a setting for shared experiences – the home as a *family* domain – has been altered.

Telephones have similarly transformed the nature of the common and private spaces in the home. The solitary black telephone in the front hallway – a location chosen for convenience and accessibility rather than for privacy – has spawned numerous generations of descendants. Phone users in the home can punch in a number from the handset or from the base, speak on a unit with or without a cord, holler across the room into a speaker phone, or, like a third of the population, use their own cellphones. Telephone company services such as call display, call waiting, conference calling, and voice mail have provided the public with the means to screen and juggle callers, link up with third parties, and access and manage banked messages with a casual ease that makes it difficult to imagine a time when such options were unavailable. Many homes today have two or three extensions on a single phone line, and many have additional lines for the kids as well as for Internet connections (not to mention separate business lines for phone and fax). With such a multiplicity of hardware and services, the typical phone user has no need to speak in hushed tones in a room with other people present. Somewhere in the home is a closed door behind which privacy on the telephone may be found.

Phones do not require special places of their own: they blend in on table and desk tops, walls and counters, and they travel around easily on people's hips or in their handbags and knapsacks. Unless someone has chosen a phone shaped like a banana or cartoon character, the telephone is next to invisible. Universal availability has expanded the range of telephone communication from a set location to every corner of the home. What was once a formal and public activity is now casual and personal. A phone call, which used to imply a particular grouping of furniture and a limited number of bodily postures, can now be undertaken while cooking or bathing, lying in bed or sitting at a desk, standing in the backyard or puttering in the garage. The provision of a basic communication service to greater numbers of people has resulted in a further separation of individual members within the home.

Video entertainment in the home has also served to isolate household members one from the other. For many critics and commentators, television has been advanced as the root cause of numerous social ills, from lazy habits and bad attitudes to illiteracy and crime. Research studies in psychology, sociology, pediatrics, and communications have examined the effects of watching television on violent behaviour, obesity, writing achievement and reading skills, hyperactivity and sensory overload in children, negative self-image, values and morals, attention deficit disorder, imaginative capacity, and analytical thinking. The results of such studies are both compelling and confusing, alternately convincing and inconclusive.

Neil Postman, in his 1982 social history, *The Disappearance of Childhood* (updated with a new preface in 1994), outlines the overwhelming effect of the electronic media, specifically television, on children and the family. His argument can be summed up in the following line: "The printing press created childhood and … the electronic media are 'disappearing' it." Postman maintains that with the invention of the printing press and the diffusion of books and book learning among the general population, a new division was drawn between those who could read (for the most part, adults) and those who could not (children). Books conveyed information, reorganized subjects, emphasized logic and clarity, and provided an authoritative context for information, all of which had been lacking on a widespread basis before the fifteenth century. Until children learned to read and join the growing ranks of the literate – a group who had been through a process of education and who enjoyed its rewards of conceptual thought and intellectual vigour – they were distinct from adults in mental ability as well as body. The invention of the telegraph by Samuel Morse in the middle of the nineteenth century, Postman continues, was the first step in the unravelling of the gains of literacy: "The telegraph eliminated in one stroke both time and space as dimensions of human communication, and therefore disembodied information to an extent that far surpassed both the written and printed word." The maintenance of childhood depended on managed information and sequential learning, and the electric communication revolution unleashed by the telegraph took away control of information from the home and school. The inventions which followed the telegraph – the rotary press, camera, telephone, phonograph, movies, radio, television – all became part of a system of communication which emphasized the graphic image over the written word and constituted a "powerful assault on language and literacy, a recasting of the world of ideas into speed-of-light icons and images."

Postman presents 1950 as the year in which the unmistakable erosion of the line dividing adulthood from childhood was marked, since by that year television had become entrenched in American homes. He explains that TV re-creates the conditions of communication which existed before the printing press, that it requires no instruction to grasp its form, makes no demands on the mind or behaviour, and does not segregate its audience. "Watching television not only requires no skills but develops no skills." According to Postman, TV challenges the authority of adulthood by merging adults and children, diminishing the wonderment of children, and replacing curiosity with cynicism and arrogance. Television undermines children's belief in adult rationality, an ordered world and a hopeful future, and the confidence in their own capacity to control violent impulses. Children adopt cynical and indifferent attitudes to political leaders and the political process, and they are introduced, via commercials, to "the joys of consumerism." Finally, Postman advances the idea that television is "an isolating experience, requiring no conformity to rules of public behavior."

However one feels about the negative or positive effects of television, one must acknowledge that it has had a profound impact on our home lives. As an appliance, the television is turned on for an average of almost seven hours a day. The average viewing time per person is four hours per day, or two complete months per year. Over a half of children aged four to six would choose to watch television over spending time with their fathers. A quarter of all people watch TV every night while eating dinner. A fifth say that they could not survive without television.

The presence of television has had an impact on the use and function of spaces in the home. Its initial invasion of the living room loosened up a room used primarily for reading, radio listening, and entertaining guests, and made it into a place where children were generally made to feel more welcome, where new levels of sound were introduced and tolerated, and where furniture was arranged to accommodate the maximum number of occupants facing a fixed object. Several people watching television together can, in certain respects, be considered as participants in a group activity, with the spectators laughing or jeering in unison and falling into conversation at the commercial breaks. But it is certainly not the same way that playing bridge, going bowling, sitting around the table at a dinner party, and other more participatory pursuits can be considered group activities. No one could claim, for instance, that they are actively engaged in a dialogue or interchange with TV. One simply *watches* TV. With a remote control, the viewer's power of choice can be executed with minimal exertion from an armchair or sofa, eliminating the need to move anything but the wrist and hand. The viewer can channel surf, watch two images at once, adjust colour and volume, and program settings without changing position.

The relative inexpensiveness of televisions and the urge to satisfy the separate, individual demands of household members has led to the current situation where televisions are to be found throughout the house, in living and family rooms, kitchens, and bedrooms. Not many people complain if they have to watch TV alone. The establishment of different viewing areas in the home, each with appropriate furniture arrangements, caters to solo viewing. It is not considered an insult if a person opts to watch a particular show in one bedroom while someone else sits alone in the living room watching something else. What was once a single phenomenon restricted to a particular location has been divided into multiple portions and distributed through the entire home.

The VCR and DVD players have expanded the entertainment potential of the television set as an electronic instrument, transforming the TV from a receiver of signals and transmitter of images into a monitor which presents the visual material stored on a videocassette or disk. The majority of households now own VCRs. The video rental store, which did not exist twenty years ago, is now as common and widespread as the corner bakery used to be. It is a shop which provides a new service to the public, a service so in demand that no neighbourhood, no major street, no small town is complete without its video hut. An average of six million videotapes are rented every day in the United States (compared with half that many books checked out from libraries). People still go the movies and pay over ten dollars to sit in a darkened auditorium with others who are eager to watch a recently released movie. In the past, if you missed a movie the first time round, you could always catch it on TV a few years later. Now, you only have to wait six to nine months to rent the movie on tape or DVD for a fraction of the cost of a single cinema ticket.

As with other shops such as grocery stores and florists, where regular patrons are on greeting terms with the shopkeepers and perhaps some of the other frequenters of the business, the local video hut has spawned its own culture of casual social friendliness. Standing in front of the movie racks, a browser of video titles can easily fall into light conversation with the stranger alongside or consult with a store employee on the merits and attractions of this or that film. Most patrons still enjoy the visit to the video hut: the pleasure of selection, the anticipation of watching the movie very soon, the atmosphere of like-minded customers engaged in a similar activity. Unlike picking up shirts at the drycleaner's, for instance, dropping in to rent a video carries with it some of the excitement of going to the movies. Once home, the eager movie watcher usually goes through a short ritual of preparation: clearing away a space on the couch, grabbing a soft blanket, bringing in some food and drink from the kitchen, setting the lights just so.

The very term "home movie" has taken on a revised meaning; it is not now the 8-mm amateur film of children and pets, screened with a loud projector for an audience who fall asleep midway through, but a movie whose title was up on the marquee and in advertisements half a year earlier, brought home in a package smaller than a hardcover book for the viewing enjoyment of a movie-goer in front of the TV. The age of video has allowed us to take a public experience and adapt it for individual pleasure at home. For a one-time investment of a few hundred dollars to purchase the necessary hardware, the enthusiast can create a personal theatre in the living room, bedroom, home office, or wherever a comfortable niche can be found for an activity which requires an uninterrupted two-hour stretch, a little peace and quiet, and a wall socket – basically, that is, anywhere in the home.

In addition to feature movies, videocassette recorders and computers play the results of our own video productions: the tapes or digital files we create with the personal video camera. Two-fifths of all households with children own a video camera, twice the ownership rate of households without kids. Replacing the 8-mm home movie camera with its bank of lights and expensive film in two-minute reels, and following on the heels of the first video generation with its bulky, on-the-shoulder camera and heavy battery packs, the nifty little videocam is designed to be held in the palm of a hand and to use tiny cassettes with two hours of tape, usually more than enough to record a birthday party or wedding. In fact, because of the generous taping time available with videocams, and the sometimes lengthy nature of the videos amateurs produce, editing of home videos is accessible to anyone who chooses to purchase an additional component for their entertainment unit or to use the video editing capabilities of their computers if they have recorded with a digital videocam.

Facilities exist in the home to recreate not only the movie theatre but the production studio as well. With a total initial layout of $2,000 to $3,000, plus the cost of the occasional purchase of videotapes, the home videographer has no need of a photo lab for lengthy and expensive processing, no huge amount of equipment to lug from place to place, no cumbersome screening procedure, and no special training beyond what can be gained from the product manuals. Technology has placed into the hands of the everyday person the means to produce a visual document which previously had required the efforts and services of a group of professionals. The complete video process, from taping and editing to viewing, can take place under one roof, produced by a single person. The days of the family gathered around the screen in the living room while Dad curses brittle celluloid and the labyrinth of unyielding spools on the projector are very much gone now. Practically any room can be chosen as a potential home theatre, and an audience of one is all that is needed to run and watch the show.

The television has become a potent tool of the advertising industry, exerting a powerful influence over the lives and homes of most North American consumers. The home has become the prime target of an ever-expanding offensive whose goal is to encourage us to adopt certain habits and buy certain products and whose vehicle for conveying this message is the TV screen. It is estimated that the average child sees twenty thousand thirty-second TV commercials in a year. By the age of sixty-five, the average viewer will have seen two million commercials. The American public has an ambivalent attitude to the advertising it watches on TV. The same proportion of adults believes that such advertising can be fun or interesting (seven in ten) as believes that commercials are a nuisance and that they encourage people to buy products they don't need. Surprisingly, only four in ten viewers switch to another station when commercials come on.

First cable and then satellite TV have set off an explosion in the number of corporations and product manufacturers on the tube, all vying for our attention and dollars. The television broadcasting industry produces over 600,000 hours of programming per year: ample time for millions of commercials. Some ads are aimed directly at teenagers and young adults (soft drinks and cars presented in the style of music videos), others at baby boomers (luxury automobiles with soundtracks from the 1960s and 1970s), and a whole new range of commercials for seniors (emphasizing the strength and vitality of many older people). The ownership of media outlets by mammoth corporations has refined and streamlined the direct link between peddlers of merchandise and the vast pool of potential buyers sitting in front of their TV sets. The global reach of the media via satellite communication has made possible the broadcast of a pitch for products and services to billions of viewers simultaneously during such mega-events as the Olympics and the Superbowl.

The intended influence of television advertising on the spending practices of its target audience can be directed towards the purchase of particular products (soda, breakfast cereals, automobiles) or services (life insurance, trade schools, temporary employment), and the viewers may respond by considering and then buying the advertised item when they next see it on the store shelves or in the shop windows. The effect of TV on consumer spending habits may also be more indirect, bringing to our awareness images not only of advertised bait but of household lifestyles which we glimpse in the programs themselves: the living room arrangements in a popular sitcom or the type of coffee-maker used by a favourite actor in a weekly show. When TV watchers open their wallets because they are either obeying the commands of advertisers to purchase their wares or picking up an idea for the decoration of their homes from the Thursday-night line-up, they are responding to a consumer urge inspired by something they saw on television.

The way a home is furnished and the products which fill it can actually be determined as a byproduct of a passive activity which takes place in front of a remarkable box plugged into the wall in any room of the home. People can design the configuration of their living environments around the presence of their television sets, which in turn parade before them an unending series of images that feed back into the consumerist loop. We welcome television into our homes and let it bombard us with a barrage of suggestions, ideas, enticements, and irresistible one-time offers to bring *more* into our lives: more toys, more tools, more food, more *stuff*.

Personal computers are a phenomenon of the last two decades which have no parallel with anything that existed before. The trusty old typewriter, made obsolete by the computer, is really the only device which can be compared in terms of function and purpose. The portable manual typewriter was an efficient and compact machine – word processor and printer rolled into one – and it took up relatively little space on the desktop. But as anyone who has used a typewriter knows, it was vastly inferior to the computer for revising and moving around text and for presenting a document with a crisp, printed appearance. Some writers still prefer their typewriters, but very few people who have used computers with any proficiency have opted for a return to the earlier technology. Three-quarters of children and teens use computers, as do a half of all adults. The age group with the highest computer usage is twelve years old: nine out of ten of them are computer literate. They will clearly not be buying typewriter ribbons as adults.

The computer as a tool for business and recreation is definitely here to stay. A few logistical issues present themselves for consideration, however. Where in the home are they to be placed – in living rooms, dens, children's rooms, home offices? And since they and their associated hardware require a basic minimum of space, will our old desks suffice or will we need a new and different arrangement to support the layout of computer, keyboard, mouse, printer and any other components (audio speakers, scanner, external memory drive) used in the home by increasing numbers of people of all ages?

Bill Gates, founder of Microsoft, in the chapter "Plugged in at

Home" in his book *The Road Ahead* (1995), sketches out his vision of how computer technology will affect us in our homes. He is sure that the information highway will not reduce the time people spend socializing, but he is eager to point out that it will create many new options for home-based entertainment, personal and professional communications, and employment. He extols the virtues of the many new activities and pursuits created by computers: on-line game playing, interactive television shows, electronic communities, and programmable functions on phones, pagers, fax machines, and computers to prescreen communications from the outside world in order to control interruptions and maintain the home as a private realm. He is also a firm believer in virtual storage: "When information appliances are connected to the highway, there will be less need for many physical things – reference books, stereo receivers, compact discs, fax machines, file drawers, and storage boxes for records and receipts. A lot of space-consuming clutter will collapse into digital information that can be recalled at will." Gates finishes the chapter with a description of his wonder home in Washington State: "My goal is a house that offers entertainment and stimulates creativity in a relaxed, pleasant, welcoming atmosphere." His faith in the benefits of the forward march of technology and in the need for people to adapt to new methods of doing things prompts him to declare: "As the ways in which homes are used change, the buildings will evolve."

Any computer in the home can be connected to the wide universe of the Internet through a simple telephone line or TV cable. More than a half of all American homes have Internet access, and nineteen out of twenty public schools are online. A third of all young people aged sixteen and seventeen spend five or more hours per week online, and the same proportion of parents think the Internet will improve their children's employment opportunities and want it to replace television in their children's lives. Although the Internet tremendously expands the range of information available to a person seated in front of a computer screen, in many ways it also narrows the field of that same user's interactions and movements. Instead of moving through actual physical space to access a library inside or outside the home, the computer user plugged into the net need only point and click with a mouse. Instead of seeking out people for face-to-face human contact, whether for social reasons or to track down a needed piece of information, net users can dispense with librarians and fellow workers in the search for facts and figures in the same way that they can forego conversation with a person seated a few feet away in exchange for a cyberchat. The more the immediate zone of a particular computer is intensified through extended use of the Internet – even if that zone is a desk in a small room – the more the world beyond that zone shrinks in significance and usefulness. It would take a special type of person to sit all day and evening in front of a computer screen, shunning the company of other people and resisting all urges to leave the room, but such a person could conceivably lead a full (if somewhat peculiar) working and social life within the confines of a single room. This, of course, is an extreme case of computer-induced seclusion, a portrait of the Internet user as a physically isolated human being. But as certain forms of the computer-centred life lead to reduced use of other segments of our wider environment, we must wonder about the effects on the spaces and facilities left behind, such as our libraries and living rooms and offices.

The use of computers and video games by children illustrates how the concentration of a particular activity in select locations around the home has led to the abandonment of other, previously popular spaces.

A half of all teens regularly play home video games and a third play computer games, while fewer than a third engage in a lower-tech, more traditional version of play, the board game. Video games have been around since the early 1970s, and shoppers now spend $5.5 billion a year on video games and related accessories and almost $3.5 billion on computer games. The most popular category of video game, listed as their favourite by a third of all players, is the fantasy violence game. The least popular category is educational, chosen by one in fifty as the favourite. Younger children still play with dolls and toys, but they are as likely to be found in front of a glowing screen as they are to be found stretched out on the floor, building a castle with wooden blocks.

Electronics have also changed the relationship between children and their outdoor physical environment. The pre-dinner hours after school used to be a time for playing in backyards, parks, and playgrounds, an opportunity for fresh air, discovery, running and jumping and hiding, a necessary break between the studiousness and discipline of school and the later evening, after dinner, when homework was done. Much of the physical activity associated with the outdoors or the basement has been replaced by sedentary electronic game-playing in the seclusion of a bedroom or a corner of the living room, either alone or in the company of a friend who awaits a turn at the mouse or joystick. Children huddle into compact areas of their bedrooms or selected portions of the family room rather than stretch their legs in the backyard or corner park. What used to be a form of punishment – "Go to your room!" or "Sit in the corner!" – is now a directive which many children follow of their own accord. As long as the room or the corner is equipped with a computer monitor or TV screen, most kids gladly leave behind the wide-open spaces of both the indoors and the outdoors for a few square feet of chair or floor.

The question of where in the home computers should be situated has as many answers as there are households with computers. A laptop can basically go anywhere. But for a full-sized computer, any reasonably sized desk which could formerly accommodate a typewriter is suitable. Wherever the desk is situated – bedroom, corner of living room, home office or study – then becomes the determining factor in where the computer goes. If householders would not put a desk in the kitchen, for instance, they would more than likely not put a computer there either. And if they're comfortable with the levels of privacy and sound in the living room to the extent that they would place a desk in such a public and accessible location, they would probably not mind having a computer on that desk. The solitary aspect of computer use would tend to indicate that the user requires some minimal level of seclusion, as much to concentrate on their own activities as not to interfere with those of others. A living room with a computer can only work if the person at the desk is not in perpetual conflict with a person on the sofa. The less public areas of the home (bedrooms, studies) are readier candidates for computer locations since they are already places where people go to be alone.

A household where more than one person uses the same computer is likely to make that facility available in a place with less private access – not in a bedroom, for example. Sharing any item or room in a home implies a degree of accommodation to the schedules and activities of others, while the more private use of separate objects and spaces generally points to a household where members are accustomed to going about their business as independent dwellers who share the public areas but retire to their own discrete zones as a matter of custom and choice. The people who value shared spaces as a defining feature of their homes will likely locate the computer centrally and openly, whereas those who view the home as a collection of private areas linked by the bare minimum of common space will tend to put their desks and computers where they themselves feel most comfortable: behind a closed door.

Householders can now take advantage of a novel device offered by home builders and designers: a communciations raceway contained within a baseboard panel which runs the entire perimeter of the home. The panel is designed by the manufacturer to enclose all telephone, electrical, and cable TV wiring, with plug-ins and jacks appearing every few feet just above floor level. This system eliminates the need to run new phone jacks or to staple lengths of cable to the wall or engage in creative extension cord wiring every time people decide to move a phone, TV, or computer. Some clever householders even channel their stereo speaker wire inside the raceway so that they can reposition their speakers or stereo anywhere in the home without having to worry about running wire over doorways and under carpets. Communications raceways give many people the uncluttered environment they want in their homes: a lean and trim style, a sense of mobility and freedom within their living spaces. The only potential drawback resides in the advent of wireless technology; will it render obsolete all previous systems involving wires, or will it too be superseded by some as-yet-undiscovered technology?

A salient feature of the new economic landscape of the past decade is the work-at-home phenomenon where increasing numbers of people have transformed part of their homes into working environments and themselves into home-office workers. The availability and affordability of personal computers, fax machines, modems, and photocopiers have, for many telecommuters and independent homeworkers, led to the decision to do away with the expense of rented office space.

By working from home, a person can economize on office costs which can then be channelled directly into business-related resources. Not only are we able to perform jobs in our homes which were formerly restricted to commercial offices, but due to the miniaturization and portability of our electronic tools, we can also continue working in our cars, on planes, on vacation, and in other peoples' homes.

Working at home is hardly a recent practice. Throughout the centuries, the line separating home and work has frequently been blurred. Using the back portion of a house for a workshop where garments are sewed or transforming the front of a ground-floor dwelling into a retail store is common in many Asian and African countries. Much of the garment industry in Latin America is located in private homes. In the United States at the turn of the century, homeworkers sewed clothing, made artificial flowers, sorted coffee beans, shelled nuts, made lace, and embroidered. Homeworkers were most commonly found in the clothing manufacturing industry where they were paid by the piece and did a small portion of the total work involved in producing a complete item. Typically, homeworkers did the same work as factory employees but they would be paid at a much lower rate. Modern communication systems have not introduced the idea of home employment but they have vastly expanded the range of products and services for which the home can serve as a base. Homeworking has changed as industry has changed. Beginning in the 1980s, workers were able to process information at home on computers and send the work by modem to the companies who employed them.

The proliferation of electronic devices for both home and office has coincided with a fundamental shift in world employment, a result of the drive for greater labour efficiency. The Industrial Revolution brought people to cities to work in manufacturing, and when assembly lines were introduced and work in factories became even more efficient, the shift to service industries began. Economic downturns in recent decades have led to massive reorganizations of employment. Lower wages in developing nations make workers in foreign countries more attractive to business than higher-paid North American workers. Larger companies also reduce their labour costs by outsourcing – that is, contracting with other companies for a portion of their in-house work, which may cover such jobs as janitorial and security, maintenance and servicing. Deregulation and the subsequent increase in competition have led to large-scale firings in many industries, as have corporate mergers. New technology has been felt most strongly in the manufacturing sector where machines can do the work of many employees without the expense of salaries and benefits. A common example of this form of downsizing is the introduction of automated banking machines and the reduction in the number of bank tellers.

Many companies hire contract employees to avoid a large permanent workforce; the employees work directly for the company (unlike independent contractors) but leave after a pre-determined period of time. Approximately seven in ten workers employed in temporary or contract positions would rather be engaged in a more conventional manner. One-fifth of our workforce are part-timers, a proportion which has increased by 70 percent in the past twenty years while the overall workforce has increased by over 40 percent. People now have an average of six or seven employers over the course of their working lives. College graduates are warned that they must be flexible, that they may have from four to six different careers before they eventually retire. The combined effect of globalization, corporate mergers, advanced technology, and staff reductions through attrition and firing has been to eradicate many jobs but also to create a new labour force: office folk who do not work in conventional offices.

Not all people who work at home are telecommuters (people who work at home but who report to an office elsewhere). Some are self-employed entrepreneurs who operate their businesses entirely from their homes, while others are employees or independent contractors who operate only partly from home and work in a central office the rest of the time. Remote call centre agents handle customer calls from home instead of from corporate locations, and virtual office workers, equipped with portable electronic baggage, can work anywhere, any-time, at home, on the road, and even in an old-fashioned office. Whatever these members of the new labour force are called – home-workers, telecommuters, home business operators – they make up roughly one-third of all workers in North America. Statisticians are hard pressed to assign an exact number to their ranks, but they esti-mate their annual growth rate between 5 and 15 percent.

The bonuses of working in a home office, in terms of bottom-line results, are encouraging: increased productivity, a higher quality of finished work, added sales, improved customer relations, flexible schedules, higher motivation, and reduced real estate costs. Telework-ers have been found to stay at the same job for twice as long as regu-lar office workers and to take half as much sick leave. The amount of time wasted in an office environment is spent, at home, on produc-tive work. (Perhaps not surprisingly, up to a half of office workers' time can be spent socializing, politicking, and game playing.) As glo-rious as working out of home may sound, however, telecommuting is not for everyone: about half of all people who leave the office are back after six months to a year. Drawbacks to home office work do exist.

Telecommuters report feelings of marginalization, isolation, and increased stress, and younger workers are cut off from the learning process that contact with other office employees provides. Some are not able to stop working when at home, while others experience difficulty with distractions and interruptions, procrastination and the inability to motivate themselves, and the lack of a regular schedule. A significant component of home work involves the redefinition of the concept of work itself. Much of our social development takes place in the context of our work lives, and if the location of our job is at home, our formation as workers will be heavily influenced by the family and the community, not the traditional office.

Two important characteristics of homeworkers are that many of them put in more than forty hours per week and that, although they have their work base at home, they also travel to other locations for meetings, to confer with superiors and colleagues, to visit clients and associates, and to deliver completed work and obtain new projects. Telecommuting does not replace the traditional workplace but rather extends and refines it to incorporate the home. Judy Hillman, in *Telelifestyles and the Flexicity: The Impact of the Electronic Home*, writes: "Today's and tomorrow's teleworkers, particularly those employed by firms large and small, may well work at home part time, at a neighbourhood office part time, from their cars or hotels when convenient, and even turn up at the main office, probably out of peak hours. Flexibility has become a key word, along with such expressions as the waking, not the working, week." Hillman adds that homeworkers are now joining the ranks of other workers such as bus drivers, waiters, and farmers who have always worked outside of the typical Monday-to-Friday, nine-to-five scheme. Working from home allows telecommuters to tailor their hours to fit their own family commitments and lifestyles as well as the working hours of businesses in other time zones and local companies who also work at irregular times.

The flexibility that comes from having a home office implies the development of a balance in our working lives between an external work environment and an internal, domestic work environment. Home offices let us work at any and all hours, both inside and outside the home. Such a degree of flexibility in our scheduling demands a corresponding flexibility in the work location at home. The question becomes: where in our homes will we work? Where do we put the home office?

Rosalyn Moran, in *The Electronic Home: Social and Spatial Aspects*, writes: "One of the major issues to emerge in considering the design implications of technological developments is the extent to which technology-related activities will take place in communal space or be conducted in more private spaces such as individual bedrooms or hobby rooms." The choice is between a single, distinct location and a home-wide distribution of facilities, with a mix of the two as a likely solution. She goes on to note, however, that separate spaces and *not* a shared use of communal space seems to be the way of the future: "Given tendencies towards increased fragmentation and diversification in use of the home it is likely that open-plan floorplans will decrease in popularity. Modern lifestyles (e.g. preferences for individual pursuits, shared use of households by unrelated persons, etc.) are best accommodated with more complete separation of spaces." If members of a household seek out private zones for play – to watch TV, chat on the Internet, or battle with space invaders on a small screen – it follows that they would also opt for a secluded area in which to do work.

Surveys reveal that although most telecommuters have a designated work space in their homes, many of them have to share that particular area with other activities. Dens, for instance, double as home offices, and many home offices double as guest rooms or libraries. The more people work from home, the greater will be their need for *more* space. With the exception of people who can design new homes with provision made especially for home offices or people who are able to convert a separate, smaller building on the property into an office, most homeworkers will either have to make an existing room share its function with the new office or they will have to convert a room for use exclusively as an office.

When consulted on the intention to modify spaces in the home for work-related use, many people express the desire to convert unused rooms such as the living room into an office. Such an admission on the part of homeworkers is revealing. The fact that some people consider the living room to be an "unused" space, suitable for conversion, implies that it may be reasonable to offer prospective homeowners a choice in the allocation of all their future spaces, specifically the choice of whether they wish to share some of the living room's space with a home office or even to devote the space in its entirety to a home office. The greatest number of future users would be served by designing a home's living space with the capacity to be easily converted, in whole or in part, to an office area *and* back again, if so desired.

The twin issues of privacy and isolation are sensitive elements in the planning of home offices. The extent to which a worker requires psychological, acoustical, and visual privacy depends on the person and often on cultural background. The concept of isolation – as distinct from privacy – depends on the level of control that the worker has over the home office environment. Privacy allows a person to work free from interruptions or unwanted observation, whereas isolation can result when the worker is deprived of desired social opportunities. The majority of telecommuters prefer a separate room as an office and they also prefer that room to be on the perimeter of the home rather than in the middle. In a room where functions have to be shared, successful accommodation is frequently made through the use of flexible and moveable items of furniture that can mark out areas in which distinct tasks are performed.

With the advent of home offices, the line dividing work life from home life has become less distinct, so we retreat further behind closed doors. The electronic paraphernalia which pervade most aspects of our domestic lives exist to improve our abilities to communicate with the great wide world. Sometimes the communication is one way, as with television, and other times we enter into a dialogue: sending out a request for information and receiving an answer by e-mail, talking on the telephone, or exchanging documents by fax or mail. The irony inherent in our use of these advanced communication devices is that although they expand the boundaries of our homes to encompass the world beyond our walls, they also serve increasingly to separate us from other people both inside and outside our homes. The more we engage in electronic activity, the more we find ourselves isolated from members of our households and the less we have need of direct contact with resources and people in institutions, offices, and libraries. We divide our homes into a multitude of private zones for individual use and we partake in fewer shared activities. Our use of the home has become fragmented; we require additional spaces for new uses and we force each space to accommodate a growing number of uses.

The home is evolving in step with the demands we place upon it. And if we approach each new change and modification with a flexible attitude – with the idea that we can eventually unmake any alteration as easily as we make it – then we provide ourselves with an unlimited stock of future options. If we acknowledge that our most recent change will be replaced by yet another variation down the line, we furnish our homes with rich potential.

From the realm of isolation and disembodied communication, we move on to a topic of communal effort and creation: the construction and renovation of our homes.

# Buy New or Renovate?

The homebuilding industry in North America is very big business. Over one million new homes are sold every year in the United States, while over four million existing homes change ownership. The construction of detached houses, rowhouses, and condominiums involves over one hundred thousand building firms who employ over four hundred thousand workers and generates $50 billion of business a year. Building homes creates jobs and stimulates the economy; the construction of one thousand detached houses, for example, produces two and a half thousand jobs and provides $75 million in wages and $37 million in taxes and fees. Every single home built requires materials and appliances, spurring the production and sale of lumber and concrete, insulation and ducting, doors and windows, toilets and bathtubs, washers and dryers. Home equity accounts for almost half of America's net worth. The total equity of homeowners in the homes they own in the United States is $4 trillion.

Despite these impressive, almost mind-boggling figures, purchasing a home is not a simple affair for many. For every rise of 1 percent in interest rates, more than four million households are priced out of the market for a home that costs $100,000. In the early 1980s almost half of all households had the annual income needed to buy a median-priced home, but today just over one-third of households earn the required amount. Money issues are not the only challenge on the home-buying front. There are well over one hundred million housing units in the United States (over eleven million in Canada), and this number is projected to climb by an additional twenty-five million homes by the year 2010. Housing production is projected to peak in 2005 when the number of households in the thirty-five to fifty-four age group reaches its upper limit at 47 million. On the other hand, by 2010 almost one-third of householders will be parents whose children have left the home, raising the demand for homes with fewer bedrooms but more leisure space. Households created by remarriage and by young adults remaining in or returning to their parents' homes will further drive the market for alternative housing configurations – homes designed for occupants other than the traditional family grouping of mom, dad, and little kids.

The average product of the North American homebuilding industry is still pretty much what most people would expect: 2,000 square feet, four bedrooms, two and half bathrooms, and a two-car garage. Most of these homes are built, not surprisingly, in the suburbs. Over the past fifteen years suburban populations have increased at ten times the rate of the city centres they surround. In general, people with higher incomes move away from high-density city centres to lower-density suburbs and outlying areas, leaving behind isolated lower-income households in deteriorating inner-city neighbourhoods or depressed rural communities. The higher-income households become homeowners and increase their wealth, while lower-income households become renters and remain excluded from the opportunity of homeownership savings.

Roughly two-thirds of homes in the United States are owned, and the same own-rent ratio holds for Canada, although the monthly costs are higher. Even with a 10 percent downpayment, the cash needed to buy a median-priced home is far beyond the ability of most renters. Homeowners spend an average of 22.5 percent of their incomes on mortgage payments, a much lower proportion than the 29 percent that renters pay. In fact, two-fifths of renters pay more than 30 percent, and one-fifth pay more than 50 percent. Of course, not all homeowners are rich and renters poor. Averages and medians smooth out the overall picture and misrepresent the many exceptions. What we can assume with a fair degree of certainty, however, is that the homebuilding industry caters to a buying public which is generally suburban rather than urban, well off as opposed to struggling. For those who live in the city centre, rent their homes, and do not earn much money, the prospect of homeownership is bleak.

The cost of buying a home has been steadily climbing over the past few decades. The median sales price of a new single-family house, for example, has increased sevenfold over the past thirty years. The labour needed to construct homes and install fixtures is far from inexpensive. (A contractor will bill over $200 a day for a skilled worker.) A typical builder will retain a small staff of secretary, bookkeeper, and superintendent, and subcontract all the other tasks of construction to avoid paying a large full-time team of workers. The builder not so much builds a house as manages the construction process. One of the builder's most important jobs is efficient coordination so that the trades arrive on site in an uninterrupted sequence. For the sequencing of trades to be effective, common guiding principles have been established: simple drawings and specifications, as well as modularity of building materials. All products assembled to form the house structure must correspond to the same dimensional system. Studs cut to a uniform height are spaced to fit a pre-cut piece of batt insulation. A plastic sheet to provide protection from vapour penetration comes in the same height as the studs. A sheet of drywall is sized to be applied to the wall framing with as little cutting and trimming as possible. Good management and modularity ensure that the construction site functions smoothly and expeditiously, resulting in the lowest possible price for the homebuyer.

The homes built today are the products of an evolutionary process which has streamlined the residential construction business. Homebuilding in the years following the Second World War can be characterized by the increased industrialization of the many practices and materials involved. Applying the speed and efficiency developed in assembly-line manufacturing, builders have adapted the same principles to the construction of homes. Complete prefabrication of houses in a factory setting has never taken off in the industry, since housing manufacturing plants have high overheads and require large orders to remain operational. Prefabricated homes have never been cheaper to produce than site-built houses. So rather than moving a house-in-progress past a line of stationary workers (as with automobiles), the industrialization of homebuilding has consisted of moving squad after squad of workers through a stationary house. Even in the immediate postwar years, it was not uncommon for up to eighteen different trades to work in sequence on a small detached house. Today, dozens of trades contribute to the building of a home, including bricklayers and carpenters, plasterers and plumbers, roofers and painters, tile layers and equipment operators, masons and electricians. A wood-frame bungalow with wood siding took about two thousand on-site man-hours to build in the 1940s, up to seven months. By the end of the 1960s, twenty years later, the same house could be built in under a thousand hours in two months. The reduced construction time can be attributed to the use of pre-assembled components and power tools as well as to the efficient movement of various trades through the house. Nowadays it still takes about two months to build a modest house, but improved building systems and products have brought down heating costs and provided the homeowner with an abundance of amenities and comforts.

The most common home built in the years following the war was the compact bungalow of about 1,000 square feet in size, smaller in fact than the two-storey detached house with a pitched roof and basement which was typical of the immediate prewar period. In Canada the federal government created Canada Mortgage and Housing Corporation (CHMC) in 1946 to help house returning veterans; in 1954 the National Housing Act mandated CHMC to administer mortgage loan insurance. In the United States the Veteran's Administration (VA) created the Veteran's Mortgage Guarantee Program in 1944 which enabled war veterans to borrow the entire appraised value of an approved house without a downpayment. Between 1944 and 1947 more than a million veterans had loans guaranteed by the VA. To be approved by the program, a family home had to be priced between $6,000 and $8,000 and to range in size from 800 to 1,100 square feet. The Federal Housing Administration (FHA), which administered the program, also mandated and controlled the style and form of allowable housing.

Postwar builders, who had to conform to government guidelines, focused on functional and economical housing solutions rather than on ornate and decorative features. Small, conservatively-styled homes became the accepted model. In terms of design, cost restrictions affected the layout of rooms. Kitchens and bathrooms were frequently placed back-to-back to save on plumbing expenses. The use of square floor plans provided a maximum amount of floor space with a minimum of wall construction. Multi-purpose rooms were introduced, to combine the functions of hallway, dining room, and living room. To economize on excavation, many houses were built on concrete slabs without basements, a practice that had been accepted during the war for factory floors. The ranch-style home was a popular form since its flat roof required less material for building. One-and-a-half-storey houses were common, with usable space in the attic, but the overall favourite was the bungalow.

The newly-built home of the 1940s had walls and ceilings finished with plaster applied on gypsum or fibreboard lath which had begun to replace wood lath. Hardwood strips were used as the floor covering, with linoleum or asphalt tile in the kitchen and bathroom. Windows, cabinets, and doors were built on site, and the interior trim was also made of wood, painted or varnished. Exterior wall cladding was clapboard, brick, or stucco. Platform framing, which uses studs only one storey in height, was the usual construction method. The roof was framed with rafters constructed entirely by skilled workmen at the building site. Insulation was still rudimentary, with vermiculite, wood shavings treated with lime, or mineral wool in the attic, mineral wool in the exterior walls, and asphalt-coated paper as a vapour barrier. Water lines were copper, with galvanized steel remaining in use for smaller pipes, and drains were still cast iron. The electrical supply to the house was typically 30 or 50 amps. Forced-air oil furnaces provided the heating, replacing coal and wood furnaces. Kitchens in these homes were small, frequently only 50 square feet, with about eight feet of counter. A single bathroom was deemed sufficient.

The bungalow remained the dominant housing form throughout the 1950s, although it had grown in size compared with its immediate postwar predecessor. By the early 1960s buyers demanded homes that were bigger and more intricately styled; the split-level became popular and was built in large numbers. Two-storey houses were back in fashion by the end of the decade, and open plans (no separation between living and dining areas and kitchens) were incorporated into most new homes. Average living space had grown to about 1,300 square feet in the mid-1960s. Windows expanded in size, with picture windows a key selling point in new homes. Double-glazed, horizontally-sliding, prefabricated aluminum-framed windows replaced vertically-opening windows with frames made of wood. Gypsum drywall was used for interior walls instead of plaster and lath. Hardwood floors were still installed, in many cases covered with broadloom; in fact, many builders began to lay the broadloom directly on a plywood subfloor. Linoleum and asphalt products were used infrequently, with plastics finding their way into many finishes and materials: vinyl floor tiles, alkyd paints, ABS (acrylonitrile-butadiene-styrene) and PVC (polyvinyl chloride) for plumbing drains and vents. The house itself was framed with smaller studs than those used in the 1940s, and prefabricated roof trusses replaced conventional rafters and joists. Exterior walls were clad with precoated aluminum or dense fibreboard sidings to reduce the amount of maintenance needed for painted wood siding. Polyethylene film provided moisture protection, and insulation values were improved with the introduction of increased quantities of fibreglass mineral wool into the roof and the walls of the basement and house frame. Electrical supply to the home was boosted: 50, 60 and 100 amps were typical services. Electric baseboard heating joined forced air as the home heating system, both made more efficient by a more airtight housing envelope (thanks to better windows and sheathing and plywood subfloors which sealed the floor-to-wall junctions). Showers became a common feature, in addition to baths, and powder rooms provided a second washroom. The kitchen doubled in size (compared with the 1940s) to 100 square feet. Counter space grew to 15 feet in length, with the surfaces finished in durable paper-plastic laminates. Solid wood cabinetry all but disappeared: plywood and veneered particleboard took its place.

The current product of the homebuilding industry is twice the size of the average 1940s home, has two stories, more bedrooms and bathrooms, and amenities unknown to the postwar dweller (recirculating fireplaces, built-in vacuum systems, walk-in closets, wide-open entranceways, double-storey spaces, to name but a few). Interior finishes have not evolved as extensively in the past three decades as they did in the first two postwar decades, although plastic and fibreboard trims are as common as site-painted wood. Waferboard, made of wood shavings compressed and glued together, is used increasingly instead of plywood for sheathing walls, roofs, and subfloors. Vinyl siding on the exterior shares the market with aluminum and hardboard. The traditional 2x4 stud used in house framing has been replaced by the 2x6, the better to accommodate thicker layers of wall insulation. Thermal insulation and airtightness have improved even more since the 1960s, with fibreglass batts the most popular insulating material in walls and blown-in cellulose in attics. Tighter windows and doors, polyethylene vapour barriers, and gasketed sill details are in general use now, all of which improve energy efficiency. Heat pumps and air conditioners are used widely, part of the reason the typical electrical service is 150 or 200 amps. The kitchen has continued to expand in size and detailing, and factory-finished cabinetry is now standard. The average number of bathrooms in a house is two and a half, and although ceramic tile is still popular with most homeowners, plastic shower-bath units are the norm. Practically all drains and vents are plastic; water lines are generally copper but plastic is widely used for these as well.

Many of the synthetic and industrialized building materials in regular use today can be traced back to wartime innovation and subsequent postwar adaptation. Plywood and drywall (gypsum board), for instance, were not invented during the war but were adopted by the homebuilding industry when there was an intense need to house wartime employees in company towns. The application of both products was found to be the quickest way to sheathe and clad houses. Plywood had been developed early in the twentieth century, but it was not until the mid-1930s that construction-quality plywood became available. Wartime need provided the incentive to bring the new product rapidly into widespread use. Aluminum siding was brought into being by aircraft manufacturers in the late 1940s who needed to find a peacetime market for shaped aluminum which had been so vital to aircraft manufacture. In order to maintain the viability of the huge factories built during the war, many aluminum housing products were introduced after the war, including siding, roofing, doors, and window frames.

Plastic production had also soared during the war years, and the plastics industry sought new peacetime uses for its products. Formica countertops, vinyl tiles, and plastic sheeting were all used extensively in the building industry during the mid-1940s and in the following years. All of these materials caught on in the housing industry because they saved money, were easy to handle and install, and reduced the time and labour involved in using them.

The method of building a home has definitely changed over the past fifty years. Tasks such as framing windows and plastering required extensive training and the execution of them was perfected over many years. Delicate finishing jobs were entrusted to highly skilled workers who spent long hours creating wood details with hand tools. Large wood sections were assembled to frame a house and the work was all performed on site. Resources were plentiful and housing demand was relatively small. Homes were firmly and solidly built, but they could be cold and drafty in winter and hot and humid in the summer. Today's homes are built more rapidly and they are equipped with a wider range of comforts and services. Although the craftsmanship in recently-built houses cannot compare with the fine detailing of former years, the techniques and materials that go into the construction of our homes today reflect the advances made in science and technology over the past decades. We are warmer in winter and cooler in summer. Rather than sheathing our new houses with planks from large-diameter, old-growth timber, we use alternative materials made from industrial wastes: sawdust and scrap wood mixed with adhesives to create fibreboard and particleboard.

Building a solid house has always involved methods that have withstood the tests of time. Building science as we know it today is, however, a recent body of knowledge. For example, the way we heat and insulate a home is as much due to advances made in the research lab as to any traditional manner of keeping ourselves warm. The wholesale use of insulating materials began a hundred years ago when houses were increasingly framed with wood. Before that time the thermal mass of masonry walls retained the heat in a way that was considered sufficient. Wood-framed walls were so relatively light and thin that some form of barrier was needed to hold in the home's heat. Early insulation included sawdust, bark and, in maritime communities, seaweed. These materials trapped warm air and retarded its escape, but they were a loose form of fill and settled easily. Mineral wool, produced by sending a blast of steam through molten rock, and slag wool, made from blast-furnace slag, were also early forms of insulation, usually stuffed into cracks and corners of the building structure. By the 1920s manufacturers of mineral wool packaged it in rolls and paper-wrapped batts for ease of use. Glass fibres ("spun glass") were produced in Germany during the first decade of the twentieth century, and fibreglass as we know it was created before the Second World War. It is still a popular form of insulation and is available in batts or as loose fill that can be poured or blown into place. Other forms of loose fill are cellulose fibre, which can be manufactured from recycled paper products, and vermiculite (expanded mica). Insulation also comes in rigid sheets or boards made of glass or wood fibre and foamed plastic, and there are methods of spraying or injecting plastic resins in a foamed liquid state which hardens into a rigid mass.

The world oil crisis of the 1970s gave a tremendous boost to home energy performance. It is now standard to insulate all walls, floors, and ceilings which separate heated from unheated spaces. The amount of insulation now required in houses is related to the climate and is measured in terms of minimum thermal resistance, or RSI value. Public awareness of the need to conserve energy (not to mention the desirability of saving money on heating and cooling bills) has led to the retrofitting of uninsulated and badly insulated older homes, the installation of double-glazed windows, and investigation into alternative energy sources such as solar heating.

An unfortunate aspect of energy conservation awareness is that, despite the fact that people replace aging single-paned windows with double-paned models (which can boost a home's energy efficiency by 20 percent) and buy energy-saving refrigerators, the overall consumption of energy is forecasted to increase by 17 percent between 1995 and 2015. Federal regulations require that all new fridges consume no more than 690 kilowatt-hours of electricity per year, almost half the amount used by fridges in the early 1980s. But when energy-saving features are extended by manufacturers and builders to the buying public on an optional basis, consumers are generally not willing to pay the extra money for the higher initial purchase in return for long-term savings. In the meantime, the main culprits in rising home energy consumption are not the larger appliances such as heaters and air conditioners but the smaller items, the assortment of home electronics which fight for plug space in most homes. The transformers (shaped like large square plugs) on appliances with remote controls and stand-by functions – which include televisions, vcrs, cordless phones, answering machines, and hand-held vacuum cleaners – suck energy all the time they are plugged in. A home with four appliances with transformers will use over 400 kilowatt-hours of stand-by electricity a year, wiping out the gains made over the past decade with energy-efficient fridges. Hot-burning halogen lamps are another energy hog, and they are inexpensive to buy and extremely popular. Householders are keen to raise the comfort levels in their homes with electronic gadgets and amenities, even at the expense of rising electricity bills.

Home security systems are another feature for which many home-owners are willing to pay for the sake of peace of mind. A solid door and a high fence used to be adequate for most people's security needs, but it is now common to have a professional electronic system installed at a cost ranging from $1,000 to $3,000, with a monthly monitoring fee of around $30. Crime statistics exist which demonstrate that home security systems actually make the home more secure against theft and invasion. The fact that they make homeowners *feel* more secure justifies their installation and expense.

As construction materials made of organic resources have begun to be replaced in homes because of resource depletion and cost-saving measures, occupants of new homes have opened their doors to a host of pollutants. Particleboard, fibreboard, and hardwood plywood are manufactured with urea-formaldehyde resins which release formaldehyde gas into the air, potentially causing skin rashes and irritations of the eye, respiratory system, and mucus membranes. Volatile organic compounds such as benzene and methacrylate, found in paints and silicone caulk, are known to cause nausea, dizziness, and headaches. Carpets and wallpaper require adhesives which contain chemical contaminants that emit gasses long after their installation. All of these materials can have adverse effects on the quality of the home's indoor air and on the health of the occupants. Alternatives to certain materials and practices are available; for example, wool and cotton rugs do not release contaminants, and adhesives can be avoided if the rugs are tacked to the floor rather than glued. Polyurethane sealants applied to particleboard and fibreboard act as a vapour barrier to seal in the formaldehyde. A balanced ventilation system in the home will always improve the air quality. Modern home construction uses more artificial ingredients than ever before, some with dubious consequences to our health. A positive way of viewing this state of affairs is to consider that we are still at an early stage in the evolution of these synthetic products and that further building science research will lead to improvements in the materials with which we build our homes and the abandonment of those which are irredeemably harmful.

Although the methods and materials used to build a home have advanced remarkably since the Second World War, the basic configuration of the North American house has changed very little. In other words, we still live and sleep in square or rectangular rooms, open doors and shut windows, turn faucets and lights on and off. The style of assembly and the composition of our homes have changed, to the extent that we rarely walk into a new house and admire the wood detail of the door frame, for instance, or the intricate carpentry that went into the kitchen cabinets. We may marvel at the spacious foyer or the number of washrooms or the size of the whirlpool bath, but we have little to say about the minute work that went into the construction. The whole system of building homes is focused on efficiency, not craft. Houses are put up speedily, with state-of-the-art materials, and they are marketed at a segment of the population that values the quantity of space, the number of square feet. Further changes, however, are in store for the American homebuilding industry: not a return to fine craftsmanship, nor an abandonment of efficient building methods, but a new look at size and at space.

The homebuying public is not the same as it was in the immediate postwar years. Their households are different, their needs are different, and they are currently engaged in a renovation frenzy. Something about their homes requires alteration, modification. It will be worth our while to investigate the renovation phenomenon so that we can better understand the direction to take when it comes to building the type of homes that best match the households who will live in them.

The market for home improvements is huge, which explains why North Americans spend almost $200 billion annually on renovations. First-time owners who are reluctant to sell their starter homes in uncertain times or who are unwilling to take on the risk of a more expensive home are choosing instead to invest in renovations. Many elderly people decide to adapt their familiar dwellings rather than move to new surroundings, opting to age in place. Some builders even leave certain features deliberately unfinished to allow the owners to make decisions on cabinetry or partitions according to their own tastes and budgets; home improvements made directly out of the householders' personal savings translate into fewer mortgage payment dollars. Increases in home sales boost the renovation market since many improvements are made either just before a house is sold or soon after it is bought. A half of all residential renovations are undertaken by homeowners in the thirty-five to fifty-four age range, and these boomers will follow the pattern of hiring contractors more frequently as they get older. As this largest demographic group in the population ages, they will spur the demand for home renovations even further.

Social attitudes to renovation are responsive to changes in thinking over time. In the decades following the Second World War it was considered normal to move on to a larger house when a family outgrew its first home or simply felt like trading up in keeping with improved fortunes. Although many households today cannot wait to abandon their starter homes and jump at the earliest opportunity to buy a bigger house, it is now considered entirely acceptable to improve the current home rather than move. There are also many personal reasons for modifying living space: the simple but sometimes inexplicable need for change ("I'm getting tired of this place – let's redo the kitchen"); the urge to express a sense of individuality ("I don't care what anyone thinks – I've always wanted to live in a emerald green house"); and the desire to exercise control over the tiny portion of the livable world that you can call your own ("I can't stand the fuzzy texture on the partitions at work, the vinyl seats on the subway train make my legs melt, and this old wallpaper in the living room is repulsive – I'm not the boss, I'm not the city transportation department, but I am the owner of this house, so get out the scrapers!").

Homeowners undertake renovations in response to life-cycle events, such as creating or rearranging space for newborn and young children, converting areas for adolescents and young adults, regaining rooms that have been vacated by departed children, and redefining rooms when a household member returns home to study or work. Households with children undergo numerous transformations over the course of twenty or more years, many of which correspond with modifications to the home. As the children get older, parents will eye spaces in the home with the intent to change, reassign, or expand. An unfinished basement which was sufficient for storage might require a make-over to function as a play zone or to contain a bedroom or two for teenagers who demand their own space and distance from the rest of the family. A room for a child who outgrows the crib and soon enough needs a desk and shelving units could be expanded or amalgamated with an adjacent bedroom, which in turn may raise the possibility of reconfiguring that whole part of the house, including remodelling the bathroom. A growing family may prompt the parents to build an addition to the house or add a storey rather than leave the familiar neighbourhood and schools, the perfect backyard, a recently renovated kitchen, and a garden and trees tended lovingly over the course of many years. Whatever the motive, householders and families will find plenty of occasions to intervene in the fabric of the building they live in. Renovation is, in fact, the active manifestation of the tension that exists between the constantly changing dynamic of living in a home and the inherent permanency of that housing structure.

Another contributing factor to the high level of home renovations is the mobility rate. In many cultures, homes and the land on which they stand are passed down from generation to generation. Houses built of stone are made to be strong and permanent. Over the years, the occupants' living habits and the functions of rooms are adapted to the fixed nature of the house because it is easier to leave the house as it was built than to move a wall. The maintenance of the home and ongoing improvements to it are made with the assumption that the dwelling will remain in the family for ever. Homes in North America are certainly not built to be temporary and to last only a few years, and many people buy houses in the hope that their children and grandchildren might live there as well. But most of us do not expect to own the same home for a lifetime, let alone hand it down to succeeding generations.

Almost one in six people move every year. Roughly one in ten owners switch homes and four in ten renters find another apartment. Most stay in the same city or town. Less a matter of personal restlessness and more a function of a restless economy, half of all movers cite work as the prime reason for uprooting themselves: taking a new job, getting transferred, looking for work. The other half move to attend school, to be closer to relatives, for a change of climate, because they have retired or are in the armed forces, and for a host of other personal and professional reasons. All of this moving results in a great deal of home renovation.

Before moving out, renovations are often made to upgrade property value. In a housing culture where homes switch hands with such frequency, renovation is seen as an investment linked not only to immediate needs but also to future plans. Putting money into a home has a dual purpose: to fix up the place and to increase resale value. Some homeowners joke that working on the house is like a part-time job. Others will claim, quite seriously, that putting time and effort (not to mention dollars) into a home is in fact a second job, that the eventual pay-off in terms of profit when the house is resold will compensate them for all the hours spent hammering and plastering which could have been spent earning another paycheque at moonlighting.

Homeowners will undertake optional work to upgrade their property, rearrange space, and add rooms or extensions; but sometimes they must enter the renovation market by necessity, to repair and maintain their homes and to replace defective components and equipment. Houses and the materials of which they are made do not last for ever. The life expectancy of the constituent parts of a house depends on many variables: the quality of the original building materials and how well they were installed, the climate, the level of maintenance over the years, and the number of different occupants and their manner of using the home. Everyone, owner and tenant alike, has had difficulty with windows at some point or other, which is not surprising considering that the average working life of wood casement windows ranges from twenty to fifty years, while aluminum casements are good for only ten to twenty. Asphalt and wood roof shingles have an average lifespan of fifteen to thirty years, wood siding anywhere from ten to a hundred years depending on maintenance, and vinyl siding fifty years. Both interior and exterior paint jobs will have to be redone at least every decade. Cast iron drain pipes last from seventy-five to a hundred years, but ABS drainage systems have not been around long enough to measure their longevity. Faucets, whether in the kitchen or bathroom, will need replacement after an average of two decades. The structural features of a house will last a long time: two hundred years for poured foundations, a hundred years for concrete block, brick, and stone walls, the framing itself the lifetime of the house. Appliances and building systems have depressingly short lives. Electric water heaters have an average life of fourteen years, gas furnaces eighteen. Major appliances last an average of fifteen years, with fridges and ovens running a bit longer and washing machines a bit shorter. Wood fences and decks require attention after twelve to fifteen years. Swimming pools, it may interest some to note, have an average life expectancy of only eighteen years. Homes are built to last but they definitely require a lot of maintenance.

When faced with the opportunity of buying a home, any prospective purchaser has two basic choices: buying new or buying an existing property. Owners of new homes spare themselves the immediate renovation work that is frequently part of the deal in taking possession of a used home. They may end up in a suburban development with saplings for trees and a distant shopping mall instead of a corner store, and they will pay the price for a brand-new house, but at least they will not have to worry about ancient furnaces and peeling paint. Those who opt for an older home may enjoy the benefits of a more urban setting (mature trees, proximity to shops and services, the pleasure of living closer to the heart of the city), and they may have bought the property precisely because it was offered at an irresistible price, but they will have to reckon with a home that may demand instant attention.

The median age of the homes in North America is twenty-eight years, and almost a quarter of all these homes are over fifty years old. Most old homes have their original foundations and framing, and many still have the same doors, windows, and floors from the time of construction. New owners of old houses generally know what they are getting into: stripping paint from moldings, baseboards, and doors, repairing cracked plaster, sanding and refinishing worn hardwood floors, replacing drafty windows, gutting plumbing and heating systems that are way past their due dates and are both inefficient and uneconomical. Renovations can be made relatively inexpensively if the owners choose to do much of the work themselves and do not mind spreading the work out over months and even years, but on the whole many big renovation jobs are not cheap: a minor kitchen remodelling averages $8,500, while a major job exceeds $20,000; the addition of a bathroom costs over $11,000; and the average price of a master suite runs upward of $35,000.

The popularity of home renovation is reflected in the recent explosion of coverage in the electronic and print media. The television show *This Old House* has been around for over twenty years, and in amongst the cartoons and religious programs on Sunday morning we have always been able to tune in and find a carpenter in his shop demonstrating the finer points of building a chair or planing and sanding a board to perfect smoothness. In their search for appealing new subjects, many family, community, and public TV channels have identified renovation as a major topic of interest. We can still find the craftsman in his workshop, narrating a step-by-step process as he moves from bench to wood supply to tool rack, but we are increasingly ushered along through a house under construction or given a guided tour of a renovation project by a media-savvy host or a smiling couple who avoid overly-technical talk and highlight the glamour.

If you get the feeling that you've seen this style of TV program before, you probably have, with cooking shows in the 1960s and 1970s and travel shows in the 1980s. Renovation was the hot ticket of the 1990s.

There are at least three dozen home improvement shows on television, including cable channels dedicated to 24-hour broadcasting of issues related to homes and gardening. There are more than forty magazines in print with the word "home" in the title. In addition to the monthlies which keep us up to date on the latest architectural trends and give us glimpses into the homes of the rich and famous, we find publications devoted exclusively to renovation and do-it-yourself (DIY) projects. Catering to the how-to market is not only a phenomenon on TV and in magazines but in books and videos as well. These products are not just meant to be Christmas and Father's Day presents given by well-intentioned spouses and children; people who work on their homes actually buy this material for information and guidance.

Our ability to use tools and perform manual tasks are indicators of the degree of our environmental competence – in other words, of how handy we are. Some people consider operating a power tool or cutting drywall with a blade to be stressful and difficult, or downright impossible, while others find it as simple as tying a shoelace. Product manufacturers have tried in recent years to demystify the use of their merchandise – whether a toilet ball or a gardening tool – and to broaden their appeal to people with limited skills. Fine print is out, numbered diagrams are in. Sometimes a piece of furniture is sold with the particular tool needed to put it together or, in the case of a larger and more complex item, with a videotape to demonstrate its application. Manufacturers and retailers are eager to make accessible to as wide a segment of the public as possible materials and products which used to be purchased only by professional tradespeople and skilled amateurs. A salient feature of the current renovation boom is the remarkable extent to which members of the middle class participate in home renovation activities. Home building requires many skills learned over the years on construction sites and is commonly the domain of workers who earn their living with tools and building products. Nowadays, an office worker who as a child may have marvelled at the fascinating implements in a carpenter's toolbox may, as an adult, own some of these tools and even use them. The carpenter need not fear that the office worker will one day steal his job. The surprise is in the simple fact that an office worker should own a cordless drill or a power saw.

Homeowners have not suddenly become plumbers who can install drains simply because they have access to magazines and videotapes. After watching a weekend show on TV and buying the appropriate manual, however, they will venture to buy new faucets and change them themselves. A huge element in this transformation of average homeowners into Mr and Mrs Fix-It is the emergence of the reno mega-store. These big-box superstores are now the top sellers in the retail home improvement market. Amateur home renovators can find everything they require in one stop: no need to visit a lumberyard, paint store, electrical and plumbing suppliers, tile store, and gardening nursery, because all of them can be found under one roof. And, it must be added, at prices that are crushing the smaller stores who cannot match the discounts of the suburban giants. The corner hardware store still exists (barely) because people value such an institution for its convenience, personal service, and the contribution it makes to the fabric of a neighbourhood. The threat to the continued existence of these classic hardware stores is understandable. The local shopper may be happy to run out and buy a package of screws or a can of paint there but will hop in the car and drive for half an hour to the big box to save money on a larger order. People will cherish the corner hardware and spend the change in their pockets for small items, but when it comes to buying a shower stall or twenty sheets of drywall they will haul out the credit card and head on over to the reno emporium.

As society becomes increasingly diverse, house builders and developers will have to rise to the challenge of constructing homes for a wide spectrum of inhabitants. Gone are the demographic and economic certainties which dictate a single housing type – the detached single-family home on a spacious lot. Such houses are still in demand, to be sure, but they do not serve the full range of potential homeowners. The planning and building of new homes and communities must provide the varied housing types that will accommodate the many preferences of an evolving population. The building industry has a long and noble tradition of making homes for people who need them. It would do well to reassess its assumptions about the citizenry who live in these homes and chart out new objectives to suit an active populace who will no sooner acquire four walls than they will busily set about changing what they find within them.

**4**

# Living with Kids

N ot all of us have children in our homes; some never will, and many have children who have grown up and left for homes of their own. But every person was once a child and that child was raised somewhere and that place was home. More than any other type of household which will undergo changes as its members move through various stages in their life cycles, families face an accelerated process of change and adaptation – a process which must be accommodated by their physical surroundings. The first two decades in a person's life present a multiplicity of challenges and transformations that take place against the backdrop of a home environment. Rooms switch function with the passing years (from nursery to bedroom to study or den and quite possibly back to a bedroom again). In the process, the rooms require enlargement or division, and they can almost always use a fresh coat of paint. Finishes are scuffed and damaged, furniture becomes obsolete or worn out, appliances need upgrading. Some spaces (like the basement) which once served only a casual purpose, must suddenly be put into service as urgently necessary parts of the home (like bedrooms for teenagers). Families often look long and hard at their current homes, forcing themselves to decide whether to move out and begin again elsewhere, or stay put but make alterations, or stay put and endure whatever circumstances prompted them to reconsider their situation in the first place. The family is the dynamic entity which generates the need for change and the home is the arena in which the changes are played out.

Specific pressures unique to our time have produced a host of new dilemmas for parents with which they must cope, both inside and outside the home. Granted, social and technological advances have done away with many unpleasant features which used to complicate and endanger the lives of children: poor sanitation and lack of medical services, inadequate education, child labour and widespread poverty, to name but a few. Parents today must deal with new challenges, the fruits of contemporary progress: environmental hazards, rampant consumerism, fluctuating domestic arrangements (divorce, remarriage, single parenting), uneven provision of education and health services, media overload, heightened awareness of crime, and a tangle of urban issues, economic factors, and government policies that have left many children and their parents with housing that is insufficient. Certain parental duties and experiences have remained constant throughout time – the need to provide clothing, food, shelter, and basic guidance for children – but many parental obligations and child-related activities have evolved over the centuries and some new variations have been created.

Let us begin our exploration of children and the home by examining the change in parental attitudes to the use of space by children. Only in recent decades have children been given the run of the home. They never used to be allowed to play in every room of the house, much less leave traces of their presence and activity in the form of toys and crafts. Children sprawling on furniture in the living room, doing homework and playing games at the dining room table, and leaving toys in the foyer are new developments in the raising of children. The use of space in a home and the rules that govern its use indicate much about the householders and their priorities. The attitudes of the occupants to their possessions and to the placement and availability of the objects within the home reflect not only aesthetic and sentimental attachments but a conception of their own place within a larger society. When parents let children know that a certain room is off limits and that they cannot touch this lamp and that bookshelf or, conversely, that they are free to play on all the furniture and handle everything within their grasp, they are transmitting personal messages about what is and what is not appropriate. Writing in a journal of developmental psychology on the subject of housing as a factor in the socialization of children, Sheridan N. Bartlett notes: "The way that available space is allocated reflects and communicates family priorities and parental intentions. Decisions about who uses what space, when, and for what purposes, are governed by understandings about such matters as privacy, decorum, identity, possession, and relationship to the wider community."

Anyone who has observed children at home knows that, left to their own devices, they will go anywhere and do anything. Some restrictions make sense: bleach and cleansers should be kept out of reach, fragile objects are not toys, valued possessions are best left untouched and in one piece, food should be kept away from upholstery, and so on. The parent who wishes to instill a sense of order and discipline by barring a child's access to a whole room or insisting that safe, unbreakable household objects are not playthings is bound to experience more frustration and anxiety than the parent who remains calm when a toddler investigates the contents of a clothing drawer or dares to enter the dining room. Laura C. Johnson, in an essay in the book *Spaces for Children* on the built environment and child development, writes that a home where the main living area "is not reserved as a showplace to be used only on special occasions, children's play is not relegated to basement recreation rooms, and kitchens are not used exclusively as food-preparation areas" is a home which conveys "the symbolic message that children and their activities are valued."

A current emphasis in accommodating a home to the presence of children is on child-proofing: installing latches on low cupboard doors, sticking plug covers into electrical sockets, removing dangerous substances and fragile items from within grasping range of little hands. An equal emphasis has also been placed on making the home child-friendly. The natural curiosity of children and their desire to observe and participate in the full spectrum of household activities requires a design concept that facilitates access to toys and all playthings, extends opportunities for discovery, and welcomes the participation of the child in everyday household goings-on. All places in the home are potential play zones to a child, and parents will do both themselves and their children a favour by expanding the range of possibilities rather than blocking them off. Phil Schoggen and Maxine Schoggen, in an essay in *Habitats for Children*, a book on the impacts of housing density, define exploration as a sequence of behaviour which answers the question, "What does this object do?" and play as an activity which answers the question, "What can *I* do with this object?" The greater the diversity of available objects in the home, the greater are the chances for exploration and play. The parent who maximizes the sources of stimulation within the home contributes to the development of children who are happy and entertained, alert and creative. The freedom to move about a home easily has been shown to have a positive effect on the development of cognitive abilities and physical coordination. Pre-school children spend an average of four hours a day playing. This is a huge amount of time for young children, and it is the time when they learn about their environment.

Parents who can supervise their children in the home with relative ease experience fewer difficulties as caregivers and find that they have to establish fewer rules. No one really wants to yell at kids all the time and haul them away from prohibited places and things. Keeping tabs on children – watching them, hearing them – is made easier when the prime locations for their activities are central and interconnected: the kitchen and dining room, the living room, and the passages that link them. Young children themselves prefer to be near adults much of the time. Still, a careful balance must be struck between the availability of spaces where the parent and child can be together and spaces where children can withdraw for privacy or rest. Hermann Zinn, in an article on the influence of home environments on the socialization of children, noted in 1980: "Research has shown that the smaller child needs both a play area for his or her activities near to the caretaker (usually the mother), and an autonomous, less-controlled, individual area, as well as the possibility of moving freely from one area to the other."

If the central areas of the home are devoted to multi-functional, child-accessible uses, with private spaces located at the farther edges of the home, a comfortable layout may be achieved. Most homes are in fact designed this way, with kitchen, living, and dining rooms at the core and bedrooms on the periphery. But if the dining room is reserved solely for infrequent meals on holidays or when guests visit, and the living room is off-limits to children because it's a showcase for fine furniture, then the multi-purpose potential of the home's focus is gone. When the central rooms in the home are considered as a single kitchen/living area with a multiplicity of functions, a large space is made available to all members of the family for play and work, meals, relaxation and visiting – whatever it is that people do when they feel welcome and at ease.

The use of the whole house by children is not, as many might think, a recipe for disaster. The kitchen can be used for family conferences and for play that involves surfaces that can easily be wiped, as well as for food preparation and eating. The table in the dining room (properly covered) is a fine surface for arts and crafts or for study. The living room, aside from its use as a TV room and a place for receiving company, is perfect for games. When access to the outdoors is restricted, the foyer and hallways are open spaces suited to more active horsing around. Sections of rooms can be designated as off-limits ("Stay away from the fax machine"). Tidiness need not be subverted ("When you're finished, put all that stuff back in the chest"). Respect for others is understood ("Keep it down – the baby is sleeping").

Access to the outdoors is an important feature of any family home for the simple reason that children like to play outside. Families who live in homes with yards enjoy smooth and easy passage to the world beyond the walls of the house. Clare Cooper Marcus and Wendy Sarkissian, in their book *Housing As If People Mattered: Site Design Guidelines for Medium-Density Family Housing*, suggest a number of guidelines for the design of yard space. They begin with the obvious requirement that the yard be visible from inside the home, preferably from a room where a supervising adult is situated. The view of the backyard from the classic position of standing in front of a window above the kitchen sink is hard to beat. Doors should be easy to use, even by a very young child, and sliding doors are not recommended for cold climates because they can get frozen shut. A small transitional area just inside the door is a good idea, to cut down on dirt and mud getting tracked into the rest of the home. The potential for the greatest range of children's play is enhanced by a variety of play surfaces within the yard itself: grass, sand, and a hard surface for toys and equipment with wheels. Enclosure is essential, but a fence should not inhibit the ability of a child to see what's going on beyond the yard. Outdoor storage space is a valuable convenience: a shed or cupboard that is waterproof, at ground level, and secure. Louise Chawla, in the article "Homes for Children in a Changing Society" in the journal *Advances in Environment, Behavior and Design*, offers the opinion that outdoor play spaces are best left unstructured. She maintains that play-oriented equipment tends to restrict rather than provide play opportunities because it stimulates only motor development and not the capacities for imagination and creativity.

Any form of housing which does not provide immediate access for children to the outdoors is a legitimate source of concern for parents. Apartment highrises are difficult for families with young children since the parents must always leave the home to supervise the children at play outdoors. Rowhouses generally have some form of yard in front or in back, or a porch or balcony. Although these spaces are smaller than the yards of detached houses, they provide the opportunity to play outside the home, supervised or not. A fine balance must be obtained on the matter of supervision: too much parental control leads to anxiety and irritability on the part of parents and a lack of freedom for the children, while too little can result in loss of parental authority and accidents among the children at play. The ability to play in or near the home comfortably and the freedom to have friends over are reinforcements with a positive role in home life.

If parents have to go outside frequently against their wills simply to oversee the children, or must cope with children cooped up indoors all the time, tension and short fuses are likely outcomes. Homes which include no outdoor space of any kind or which have areas too small to accommodate boisterous and exuberant play benefit from a cluster arrangement where the backs of many homes open onto a large common space. When a parent can stand indoors and confidently watch children outside, it hardly matters whether the kids are in a private yard or a larger park-like setting. Children raised in city centres find nothing odd about shared facilities in nearby playgrounds. They might even be baffled to discover that in other areas of the city there exist adjacent yards, each with its own swing-set to cater to children who play separately and alone.

On the matter of outdoor children's play, we would be remiss if we did not take a moment to discuss the issue of child safety and crime against children, especially as the topics are sensitive elements of current public consciousness. It is sometimes difficult to know whether we are living in a time which is no more dangerous than any other or in a foul age which is particularly nasty and fraught with peril for youngsters. The media concentrate hungrily on crime involving children, and the bare statistics are sobering enough. Almost one-tenth of all prison inmates are serving time for victimizing a child. One-fifth of prisoners convicted of violent crime have committed the crime against a child, in half the cases against a victim under twelve years old. One in ten murder victims is someone under the age of eighteen. "Streetproofing" is a new word in our modern lexicon, and there is no shortage of books, police workshops, and child advocacy groups that teach parents about situations with which their children ought to be familiar, from dodging strangers' questions to escaping if abducted. Parents today know that things are different from when they were kids. Children are allowed to go into public alone at a much later age than formerly, and parents are now far more cautious in the surveillance of their kids.

Even inside the home, parents now seem to take extra precautions, perhaps because the contemporary home is a repository for so many potentially dangerous substances and objects. Household safety books and parenting magazines offer numerous instructions on how to childproof a home, and government agencies produce literature on child safety with regard to cars and household appliances and equipment. Magazine articles also focus on the prevention of injuries to children at play (bicycling, rollerblading, sports). A parent will naturally act to keep a child out of harm's way, but the level of vigilance required nowadays indicates either an excessively worried generation of parents or a society and environment that present a surfeit of potential pain as the unfortunate side-effect of social and technological advances. Whatever the cause, wary parents know that both inside and outside the home they must guard against dangers that run the gamut from caustic cleansers to suspicious strangers loitering at the school fence.

We return to the subject of children's play. The spaces within the home that have officially been designated as rooms for children are a recent appearance in the history of home. With the increased acceptance of the idea that the whole house is adaptable to the entire family's use, indications point to the eventual disappearance of these places as zones specifically for children. In the 1920s heating manufacturers suggested that the basement could be converted into a recreation room now that furnaces were more compact. After the Second World War, multi-purpose rooms became popular in new homes. This non-living-room went by a variety of names until a parenting magazine in 1947 dubbed it the family room. Many of the parents of young children today – those who grew up in relatively new detached houses – spent much of their own childhood in basement rec rooms or watched TV in a family room rather than risk messing up the formal living room. These parents may live in the same type of houses and may very well see the benefits of having a space in the house just for kids. But since many of these parents have opted, out of necessity or choice, to live in homes where every square foot must perform double or triple duty, the assigning of a separate area exclusively for children might be less efficient than incorporating the activities of the kids into all the other areas of the home.

Not all of a child's life is fun and games. Children aged five to seventeen do have plenty of free time, which is to say, time not spent at school and on homework, eating, bathing, in transit, or asleep: an average of seven hours per day. Children aged five to eleven spend three of these hours at indoor play and two watching television. Teens (twelve to seventeen years old) play indoors for an hour and a half and spend three hours watching television. School is the first major non-play activity in the lives of most children, and it consumes a healthy chunk of their days: kids aged five to eleven spend an average of five hours on weekdays on school and homework, while teens (twelve to seventeen) spend seven hours. Just how much time children spend on homework is unclear. Whether in grade four, eight, or eleven, most students appear to spend less than an hour a day on homework. A full quarter of all students claim that on any given day no homework has been assigned. It would be safe to assume that elementary and high school students spend anywhere from no time at all to a maximum of two hours a day on assignments done at home.

The whole issue of homework is complicated by the use of computers by children. For example, does an hour of web browsing for information needed for a school project, interspersed liberally with excursions into non-school-related web territory, still qualify as an hour of homework? Regardless of how time is spent at the computer and which sites are accessed, this new mixture of schoolbooks and CD-ROMs, pencils and keyboards, rubber erasers and delete functions has widened the scope of both the materials and the space required by children for their schoolwork at home.

In the pre-electronic age, homework was a straightforward affair: it was performed with books, paper, pens and pencils at a desk in a bedroom or at the kitchen or dining room table. The same objects and locations are still used today, but many more tools have been added (computer, Internet connection, scanner, fax) and additional areas of the home are involved (a parent's study, the living room, the den – wherever the electronics are situated). Children do not need huge desks and larger bedrooms simply because they use computers, nor do they have to monopolize the more public areas of the home because the computers are there. The prime consideration for parents of school-age children is to realize that their kids' homework-related needs differ from what theirs used to be, so they should allocate the space in their homes accordingly. If this means laying out the living room, for instance, to accommodate watching television, reading, lounging, *and* doing homework, then at least future squabbles can be avoided (or at least reduced) through family scheduling and compromise. Placing a computer in the living room in itself implies a new, expanded use to the space. If such an arrangement is not suited to the way the family operates, then another solution must be found. The innovative aspect to planning and layout of this kind is the fact that it happens at all. Pretending that a home can be designed, furnished, and used as it was fifty years ago is impractical. Tallying up the potential uses and assigning effective multi-purpose spaces is a strategy more in tune with current demands.

The way a family forms and operates is itself an intriguing concept. Two people who have grown up in separate households with different lifestyles and habits join to create a new household. Each person brings unique experiences, tastes, and traditions to the relationship. Together they form a bond with mutual goals and dreams, and they then produce children for whom they have provided a family home. These children will eventually grow up and repeat the cycle, forming their own pairings and households and raising their own children. This is society's traditional pattern, the blueprint for families that has been used for generations.

Not all children, however, are brought up in households which conform to this plan. Statisticians define a family household as a home with a married or unmarried couple or a single adult living with their own child or children. Separation, divorce, and never even getting married are common features in the contemporary family landscape. When people speak of "family values" they are generally referring to the values (whatever these may actually be) which pertain to the married-couple family and to an ideal lifestyle they are presumed to exemplify. Not until society as a whole comes to recognize that *all* families make up the complete constituency of parents and children will people begin to acknowledge the diversity of family types. And when diversity rather than a single model is recognized as the norm in dealing with all aspects of family life, perhaps then a new mode of thinking will govern the myriad concerns relating to the family and children, from role models and social expectations to employment and housing.

In 1947 only two in ten married women worked outside the home. Over the course of the intervening years, that proportion has shot up to seven in ten. The difference in home life for children at the present time compared with those in the immediate postwar years is obvious; many more children are now cared for during the day by people who are not their mothers. One-third of all children whose mothers work full-time are in pre-school or daycare. The significance of this movement of so many young children out of the home and away from their mothers is still contentious. Some parents feel that working mothers and children attending daycare are at the core of the decline of the family. Others consider that two working parents or a working single parent are an economic necessity, that without the income there would simply be no home or family. Yet another group of working mothers (those with the ability to choose whether or not to continue working) have felt the pressure of a career on the functioning of the household and have opted to give up their job and stay at home with the kids. And some couples have decided to turn the traditional family model inside out and have dad stay at home with the children while mom becomes the sole breadwinner.

However the situation is interpreted, parents find themselves in a working society markedly changed from the time of their grandparents. The effects on the use of the home are as varied as the assortment of domestic arrangements. It could be argued that with fewer children at home there is a reduced need for child-related spaces and facilities. On the other hand, children past a certain age have always gone to school for a portion of the day, and no one has called for fewer resources in the household for children just because the home is empty for many hours. And although children may be tended by adults who are not their mothers, many of these kids remain at their own homes in the care of others while the parents are away. It is difficult to ascertain just how empty or full family homes are during the daytime, and one might wonder if the issue even has an impact on the distribution of uses in the home. The priority for parents is to analyse their own particular situation with regard to the spaces they inhabit, to create functional households that best suit their current needs, and to remain open to changes in the use of their homes as dictated by inevitable changes within the family itself.

Parents of grown-up children cannot reasonably expect that when their kids leave home they will stay away for good or, for that matter, that they will leave at all. Almost half of all parents in their forties and fifties have an adult child living at home with them. Since 1960 the number of people aged twenty-five to thirty-four who live with their parents has more than doubled from two to five million. These stay-at-home adults also include offspring who have left the parental home only to return later. During the Second World War and the subsequent baby-boom years, one-third of adult children who left home for at least four months returned to live with their parents for at least another four months. That proportion has since risen to two-fifths. Home-returners are made up of divorced adults with their own children who need a place to stay after the dissolution of their households, grown kids who have failed to make a go of it on their own, and college graduates who are not yet ready financially to establish a household by themselves. Parents with young children who assume that their families will follow the traditional pattern – kids are born, grow up with the parents, leave home at around age twenty, return to visit with their own children for holidays and Sunday dinner – may be in for a jolt when they find, for example, that a son takes up residence in the basement and makes no effort to leave, or a very young daughter becomes pregnant and then continues to live in their home with her new baby.

An increasing number of children live in a three-generation household not headed by their own parent: some live in a household headed by a grandparent, others live with at least one parent in the home of the grandparent. The growing evidence of multi-generational domestic arrangements indicates that the old-style extended family may be making something of a resurgence in North America. When adults of different ages and children share the same home, certain accommodations must be made by everybody to deal with competing expectations and conflicting claims on the use of particular spaces. Adults who are not the primary householders will demand control over private areas. The bedroom for one person may be turned into a study, only to be transformed back into a bedroom for a young parent with a child. If, from the outset, a family concocts a twenty-year plan that includes moving through a series of homes, each one corresponding to an expected change in household composition, that family may be in for a measure of frustration and disappointment. Better to choose with care a home that will evolve with their rising and falling fortunes, their certain changes and their surprise events, a home that rolls with life's punches.

The process of growing up involves not only the shedding of many childish characteristics but the acquisition of adult-like traits, including the desire to claim space. In a time when, owing to the wide-open nature of the media and the Internet, children gain access to an aware-ness of the world of adults at an earlier age than their parents or grandparents ever did, the emphatic presentation to parents of notions such as the need for private space can sometimes come as a bit of a surprise. Nevertheless, teenagers have always made claims for rooms of their own. They want a place where they can put up their own posters, play their own music, arrange things the way they want, and establish their own rules. If the entire home can be considered as the domain of the household, and the family has a perceived right to such a domain within the larger context of other homes and house-holds, the older child feels justified in carving out a slice of the fami-ly portion as a miniature private domain. Since the bedroom is often the only place older children can call their own, it is essential that it be a room outfitted for multiple functions: a place to sleep, do home-work, store things, and spend time with friends.

The allocation of bedroom space in the home is a matter which can be less straightforward than is generally taken for granted. Sheridan N. Bartlett, in his article on the socialization of children, for instance, raises the issue of sleeping arrangements for young children and cites an anthropological study which investigated child-rearing practices in twelve communities in different countries. The researchers found that infants routinely sleep in cribs in their own rooms only in the United States where the culture places a high value on independence and considers that development towards autonomy would be retarded by reliance on other people during the night. Louise Chawla notes that children (of whatever age) with their own bedrooms are found to play in more varied and imaginative ways than children with shared bed-rooms and are also more likely to entertain their playmates than their shared-bedroom counterparts. Individual bedrooms are, in fact, favoured by most parents; a room with dimensions of at least 10 x 15 feet for each child is the preferred size.

The never-ending desire for more space or a larger home could be alleviated if parents did not feel under pressure to provide a separate room for each child from the earliest age. Sleeping with other young siblings in the same bed or room is not inherently unnatural. When large bedrooms for each child are unavailable, it is preferable for two small children to share one large room than to have their own smaller rooms – an arrangement which provides both of the children with more space to play in their private section of the home. Teenagers, on the other hand, benefit from having their own rooms, no matter how small. Unlike infants and younger children who want and need to be near their parents, teens crave autonomy. Designing homes with fewer but larger bedrooms which can be partitioned as needed makes more sense than yielding to the present custom of measuring a home's capacity and quality on the basis of its number of bedrooms. Parents with three children who look for a home with no fewer than four bedrooms may be burdening themselves with unnecessary frustration and expense.

The subject of large and small bedrooms raises one last issue with respect to housing families and children: residential crowding. Homes built in a setting more dense than neighbourhoods of detached houses do not in themselves create a crowded environment. The effects of housing density vary immensely, depending on a number of factors: the type of unit (apartment, rowhouse, plex), the layout of the home (tight or open), the location (urban or suburban, pleasant or dismal neighbourhood), social and cultural background of the householders (comfortable with dense surroundings or miserable and resentful), availability of open outdoor spaces, number and ages of the children. Young parents living downtown with one or two children in a 1,000-square-foot rowhouse may be happy and proud of the way they live, with no urge to leave the heart of the city and move to a higher-maintenance, more expensive home in a neighbourhood far from the conveniences they have come to take for granted. On the other hand, parents who live in an apartment complex in a cramped space accessible only by a long elevator ride, and who spend their lives at home cursing the tiny rooms and the absurd placement of walls and their neighbours, and who would rather live anywhere else, probably have a different opinion about density.

True crowding is a problem quite apart from residential density and not simply a trick with words to mask identical situations. Under crowded conditions, where people experience the worst effects of limited space combined with an inadequate arrangement of that space, life can definitely be unpleasant. Unacceptable noise levels, lack of privacy, excessive and unavoidable exposure to other household members, constant movement in the hallways and rooms are all undesirable consequences of crowding. Communication between parents and children is compromised because of intensified contact. Family conflicts are easily exacerbated, positive stimulation is blunted, levels of irritability and frustration rise, and parents resort to harsher forms of discipline to control behaviour which can be, in many cases, normal and inoffensive. Parents who live in bad housing are more likely to be abusive to their families. Children who have few opportunities to put some distance between themselves and other siblings or their parents are likely to feel the strain and respond accordingly: they misbehave, become moody, and cope as best they can with unsatisfied desires and needs.

In common with other negative circumstances in life, crowded living conditions produce varying effects, depending on the attitudes and values of the people involved. Parents can make matters either better or worse for their children in a crowded home. Alan Booth, in an essay on family interaction and household crowding in the collection *Habitats for Children*, writes: "If relations between family members are already poor, crowding will result in further decrements. If family relations are rich, compressed living conditions will enhance them." It may be of little comfort to those who live with too many others in too small a space, but people who have lived with crowding for a longer period generally cope better than people new to the situation. Booth notes that "if crowding does have an effect, it is short-lived, as people accommodate their lives to their surroundings." The qualifier "if" is interesting: it would seem to imply that crowding may in fact have no deleterious effects. Lorraine E. Maxwell, in the article "Multiple Effects of Home and Day Care Crowding" in the journal *Environment and Behavior*, is not so equivocal. She reports that the academic performance of children has been found to be adversely affected by crowding in the home, the main cause being the inability to find a place to study away from the activities of others. A prerequisite for efficient study is a "functionally private" space: a location that may have many uses over the course of a day but that can be devoted entirely to a task such as homework when needed. Maxwell goes on to cite other negative effects of crowding. Children living in crowded homes are more aggressive and distractible in school. They tend to retreat inward to find privacy, becoming secretive and unwilling to share thoughts and feelings with parents. They tend to play alone more frequently and avoid interactions with others. These children also spend an inordinate amount of time outside the home.

For many parents, the image of the ultimate family home includes wide streets, lawns and driveways, a garage for two or three cars, and a house with a bedroom for each child, bathrooms everywhere, a master bedroom to rival a hotel suite, a grand foyer, a finished basement, and a kitchen in which to prepare feasts (not that feasts are at all a regular occurrence, but just in case). Some people want and can afford homes like these, so they buy them and live in them. Others dream about such places but never achieve their dream. But a great many people have realized that it would be pointless to entertain even the possibility of such a scenario. The expensive house is not for them: too costly, too unsuited to their needs, not at all what their lives require. A "family home" is not another name for a "dream home." It is simply a place for parents and children to live happily. That place could easily have a 20-foot frontage and 1,200 or 1,500 square feet of space on two levels. The children could be within walking distance of their schools and not need to be driven by school bus or car pool. The priority in finding a home should not be the pursuit of an unsuitable or unattainable goal. Obvious as it may sound, the focus should be on finding the right kind of home and on using it well.

Finding the right kind of home involves two important considerations: choosing a place which suits current needs and budget, and one which has the flexibility to adapt to potential changes down the road. A forty-year-old baby boomer who grew up in the 1960s, for example, may have lived in a large house with many siblings. Dad worked, mom stayed at home, the mortgage got paid. This same boomer may now have two children and a wife who also works at a job with as little long-term security as his own. The four-bedroom house he grew up in may now cost over $250,000: too expensive and too big. Besides, boomer mother and boomer father haven't lived in any home larger than 1,500 square feet for the last twenty years. They will look for something smaller than the homes of their youth, and considerably cheaper. And since they are settling for a home where every square foot counts, they want to be sure that they can amalgamate two small bedrooms into one and then split them apart at a later date, that the study can accommodate laundry facilities or space for storage, and that the den or family room can be whatever they want it to be. They want to feel that they've bought a house which will do their bidding and be able to change with them over the years. A bedroom will eventually become a study but may need to become a bedroom again some day. These same boomers, fifteen or twenty years later, may have to provide a room for one of their children for longer than they had expected. They may think all the kids have left home, only to have one of them divorce and return with children. They want to be ready for what life offers and they want a home that reflects that readiness.

Multi-functionality is the strategy for making maximum use of any space. Parents who are used to rigorous scheduling in their work lives or to balancing the infinite demands placed on them by their kids should be able to allocate uses for the rooms in their homes with a reasonable degree of efficiency. Many parents have joint custody of their children following a split and may not have space for a bedroom that is used for only part of the week or on weekends. Without depriving children of a special area of their own, these parents can make certain rooms perform double duty in ways that do not force a child to sleep on a couch in the living room. A multi-purpose room in a father's apartment can easily be laid out to contain a bed for a child, shelving for storage, even a washer and dryer. Studies and home offices can make interesting weekend bedrooms. Using your home well means using every last bit of it, not wasting rooms for infrequent activities. Using your home well also means letting the children use it, too.

There are too many variations on the traditional family to believe that a basic family home can satisfy everybody. Each family is unique and each home is unique. Even so, all families share many concerns. Parents want to provide their children with care and with love, and they must also be practical. They balance child care and work, grocery shopping and mortgage or rent payments, toy purchases and credit card bills. Children spend time in schools, shopping malls, the great outdoors, but home is where they live. Home is undeniably the focal point of family life. A family could be a father and his teenage son, or two parents and their five young children, or a woman in her sixties who lives with her forty-year-old daughter and two grandchildren. Their homes will be different, as well they should be. But they all need a home, and they all want a good home, the best home they can manage.

# Growing Old at Home

Researchers into the subject of aging use a chart called the age-loss continuum to present the milestone events which correspond with the stages of life from fifty years onward. Displayed as a figure in an article or a book, the simple chart readily captures the reader's attention: one is surprised, perhaps shocked, to see the latter part of the life cycle reduced so efficiently to the basics. The age-loss continuum reveals that, on average, we are separated from our children during our fifties; we lose our regular incomes and jobs, suffer a diminishment of sensory sharpness, and endure the death of spouse and friends at the age of sixty-five; experience a drop in motor activity at seventy-five; and finally undergo a serious deterioration of health, physical mobility, and independence after the age of eighty. (Mercifully, the word "death" is not to be found at the end of the chart, presumably because it is far too obvious to require a mention.) The age-loss continuum shows us what we all know and what many of us dread. It reminds us that aging is a continuous process that becomes more noticeable the older we get and the effects of which are more debilitating in the later stages.

The younger a person is, the more difficult it is to accept and comprehend the notion of growing old. In the midst of a healthy and active life, a young person rarely thinks about needing a cane or being incontinent or undergoing a hip replacement. The last thing a young person cares to consider is the prospect of not hearing parts of a conversation, or having trouble turning the pages of a book, or feeling confused and helpless, or tripping because of poor depth perception. Of course, these examples of failing ability are not exclusive to advanced age nor are they certainties for all older people. So much concerning a person's physical and inner states depends on genetic inheritance and lifestyle, on decades of good and bad habits, and on energy levels, attitude, and plain luck. Some characteristics of age are natural and unavoidable, others seem to be subject to fortune and chance.

The life expectancy for a child born in 1900 was only forty-seven years. Over the course of a century, that figure has risen almost thirty years to seventy-six (seventy-three for men, eighty for women). If a person reaches the age of sixty-five, life expectancy is even higher: eighty for a man, eighty-four for a woman. People are simply living longer than they used to. The implications for society are clear: since people are living to a later age, a greater proportion of the whole population will be made up of older people. One in eight of all people in the United States and Canada is over the age of sixty-five. By the year 2030 that proportion will have shifted radically to one in five. The major reason for this swelling in the number of elderly people (aside from improved health care and nutrition) is the aging of the baby boomers. Between the years 2010 and 2030 this huge group will turn sixty-five. We must also bear in mind that the future composition of society will include not only greater numbers of old people but older old people. By the year 2030 one in ten people will be over seventy-five, the same proportion in 1970 for people over sixty-five.

Since the number of old people is increasing at a greater rate than that of the overall population, we may naturally wonder how these swelling ranks of older people will care for and house themselves. At present there are three working people for every person over the age of sixty-five, but by the year 2030 that proportion will have changed to two-to-one. A different way of referring to a similar phenomenon is expressed as the "parent-support ratio": the number of persons over the age of eighty-five per every hundred people aged fifty to sixty-four. In 1950 this figure was three, at present it is ten, and by the year 2050 it is forecast to be almost thirty. Less scientifically, perhaps, yet more simple is the finding that one-third of the oldest baby boomers report that they are presently or will be supporting both children and parents. But the question remains: Who will support all the other aged parents? Do they, in fact, require support?

The whole issue of discussing the needs and care of older people is linked to the vital consideration of ascertaining exactly who are the subjects under discussion and how we are to refer to them. For instance, what do we call this massive demographic group who have in common only the fact that they are all sixty-five years of age or older? We (the authors) have decided to avoid terms like "senior," "mature," and "golden," judging them to be inexact, inappropriate, and in fact condescending. On the other hand, words like "aged," "elderly," and "old" may seem harsh to some or even unsuitable. In our own notes for this chapter, we used a simple shorthand notation to signify our subject group, a quick three-character name without value judgment or subjective connotation: 65+. For the sake of the present discussion, however, we have found it necessary to refer to 65+ by more recognizable terms – words which we hope will not give offence or create confusion, such as "people over sixty-five" or "the elderly" or even just plain "old."

As for the question of what qualifies a person for inclusion as a subject of discussion in this chapter, we have decided to use the age of retirement as determined by German chancellor Otto von Bismarck in 1875 when he created a pension policy and by the Social Security Act of 1935 in the United States and by the Canada Pension Plan, namely sixty-five years of age or older. Defining old can be a very tricky issue indeed. One in three people in their twenties think that people are old even before the age of sixty-five, while only one in fourteen people in their sixties would agree. For those under thirty, old is somewhere around the age of sixty-seven, whereas for someone over sixty, old does not begin until seventy-seven. The average age at which a person is considered old – the age agreed upon by people of all ages – is seventy-two. Still, everyone knows that the segment of the population over the age of sixty-five is a highly heterogeneous group composed of people with varying tastes and abilities and different preferences and needs. A person of sixty may be cantankerous, inactive, and sick, while a person of eighty may be healthy, positive, and busy. No single definition or age could possibly encompass such a vast array of the population, such a wide selection of lifestyles and birth years, dispositions, and physical characteristics.

One more item which must be highlighted in any discussion of the elderly is the extent to which women outnumber men, especially at later ages. There are five women in their late sixties for every four men the same age, five women for every two men in their late eighties, and four women for each man in their late nineties. Over half of all men die as husbands with a surviving wife, whereas only a quarter of women die as wives with a surviving husband. Four-fifths of all people over sixty-five who live alone are women. And two-thirds of people who die at the age of eighty-five or over are women. On the whole, women simply live longer than men. All people get old, and most matters relating to the elderly apply equally to men and women, but when it comes to distribution of numbers according to gender – whether with reference to housing or to any other social phenomenon – it is important to recognize that many more older women are involved than older men.

To better understand the modifications to our homes that are undertaken as we age, we would do well to examine the changes that occur to people past the age of sixty-five. These changes can be broadly divided into two categories: personal/social and physical. In the first category, we include all the emotional, spiritual, and psychological transformations that affect the lives of people as they get older. Since most people take the personal and social needs of many adults for granted and take no note of them until they are withdrawn or diminished, it is important to recall them consciously when an older person's capacities and independence are in decline. They include (in no particular order) the need for friends and family, a sense of belonging and continuity, intimacy and privacy, opportunity and choice, leisure and stimulation, achievement and status, and a measure of autonomy.

As difficult as it may be to identify or even acknowledge some of the disorienting and painful aspects of aging, researchers have attempted (with varying levels of success) to pinpoint certain effects of growing old on the inner feelings. Leon A. Pastalan, in an article entitled "Sensory Changes and Environmental Behavior," writes: "The most impressive finding was the occurrence of an emotional paradox. A feeling of being strongly insulated from the rest of the world was complemented by the feeling of vulnerability to the rest of the world. The outside world seemed to be farther away and, at the same time, more threatening. Elements comprising the feeling of insulation included a preoccupation with bodily sensations, greater amounts of time spent in fantasy, and reduced social contact."

Pastalan goes on to describe the feeling of uncertainty in social situations and of the potential embarrassment and anxiety caused by "smiling to someone with no idea of whether or not that pleasantry was being reciprocated, speaking in earnest with no assurance that the listener was paying attention, and trying to interact with no feedback." These types of situations are not only stressful in themselves but prove to be disincentives to further social contact.

Polls and studies provide a number of findings on post-retirement living with which most people would agree: the elderly have a greater number of free and available hours, they spend more time on housework than younger people, and also engage in more religious and volunteer activity than the general population. People over sixty-five are frequently able to devote time and dedication to hobbies and tasks they might not have been able to pursue at an earlier age, such as gardening, quilting, or genealogy. Similar to people of all ages, older people respond to life events in a variety of manners: withdrawal or indulgence, exultation or resentment, acceptance or denial. An emerging characteristic of the baby boom generation is the tendency to resist the aging process or at least to redefine the social connotations associated with aging so that their senses of identity and self-esteem will not be adversely affected as they grow older to the same extent as their parents' and preceding generations. One thing all people experience the older they become: as control over life decreases, as elements of certainty recede, as independence fades, the concept and reality of home assume increasing importance. When everything seems to be falling away, the central position of home acquires added significance in life.

The physical impairments that occur with advancing age are inevitable. The only question for each person is to what extent his or her body will be affected and at what age the changes will happen. Approximately one in ten people in their late sixties requires assistance in some form to overcome physical limitations, and roughly half of all people over eighty-five need such help. The design of the home for an elderly person must take into consideration the many activities of daily living, all of which involve the condition of the body: bathing, dressing, walking, bending, kneeling, reaching and so on, which depend upon strength and balance and coordination, mobility and agility, seeing and hearing, smelling, tasting, and touching.

To give an indication of the prevalence of the physical impairments which come with age, it would be helpful to note some of the problems older people have with basic activities. One-third of all women in their late sixties and early seventies have trouble lifting or carrying twenty-five pounds, and one in ten cannot lift or carry such a weight at all. One in ten in this age category has trouble with only ten pounds. A half of all people over the age of sixty-five experience some difficulty with grasping. One in four have trouble reaching overhead, and three out of twenty are unable to. When one realizes that health and nutrition, hygiene and safety, not to mention the basic ability to get around all depend on the state of the body, one begins to appreciate the extent to which the "friendliness" of the physical environment plays a role in the independence of an elderly person.

The five senses all take a beating in later age. The problems with vision are many: a reduced ability to adapt to changing light conditions, increased sensitivity to glare from abundant natural light and unbalanced artificial light, faded colours, inability to distinguish blue from green, diminished peripheral vision, difficulties perceiving the boundary between contrasting surfaces, blurring of fine detail, and inadequate depth perception. The need for stronger lighting is acute: a person of sixty needs three times the amount of light that a twenty-year-old needs to accomplish the same task. Hearing loss can begin early, even with people in their fifties. Roughly three in ten people over sixty-five have serious hearing problems. Difficulties with hearing include a decreased ability to hear high-frequency sounds, problems with hearing conversation clearly when there is noise in the background, missing words and parts of words, and experiencing trouble with identifying or locating sounds. The senses of smell and taste are related, and the impairments associated with advancing age include a reduction in the taste of food and in the pleasure of eating, and a curtailed ability to gather information (sometimes subconsciously) on the immediate surroundings, such as smells from various parts of the house or neighbourhood and danger signals such as the smell of seeping natural gas. The sense of touch is also affected adversely by age; this includes an increased sensitivity to light touch, a greater risk of frostbite and burns (due to difficulties detecting temperatures), problems with differentiating textures, and hand-eye coordination deficits.

Older people are also more liable to break bones through loss of bone mass. Compressed vertebrae and sunken foot arches lead to a shortening in height and sometimes to a hump on the back that makes reaching and looking upward difficult. Joints become stiffer with age. Hips and shoulders degenerate and sometimes require replacement.

Finger joints stiffen and become painful. Muscles shrink and get tougher, making all forms of activity more problematic. Sleep does not come as easily for older people as it does for most younger people, and the elderly wake up several times a night to go to the bathroom. Advances in science and technology have prolonged life and alleviated many of the depredations of age with the introduction and routine application of surgical procedures and medical treatments, transplants and implants, operations and drug therapies. Public education has been linked to lower levels of physical disability. Exercise and healthy living have become widespread and even fashionable. But age and disease, however they may be fought or delayed, will overcome us all eventually. Our living environments must be adapted to facilitate our sometimes uneasy advance into our later years.

Despite the numerous impediments set up in our path as we age, the overwhelming majority of people prefer to remain independent and to live at home rather than move in with a relative or enter into an assisted-living arrangement. In an article entitled "Living Independently with Neighbors Who Care: Strategies to Facilitate Aging in Place," James T. Sykes writes: "Over time, the significance of 'home' increases as older people face the loss of other symbols of independence and connections to the mainstream of life. Nearly every study affirms the conventional wisdom that older people strongly prefer to age in place, to grow old within familiar territory that has provided a context for their lives, whether they live in single family dwellings, elderly housing complexes, or naturally occurring retirement communities." For many, the prospect of moving into a nursing home is horrible and only considered as a last resort.

Although family, friends, and neighbours are instrumental in helping older people maintain their independence, many people over sixty-five consider living with their children to be unacceptable since it creates conflict and turns them into a burden. Three decades ago almost 30 percent of all Americans over sixty-five lived with their children, but today that proportion has halved as ideas about independence have changed. For instance, almost all baby boomers want to retire before the age of seventy, and one-third want to quit working before sixty. In contrast, three-quarters of workers already in their fifties and sixties expect to be working past the age of sixty-five. Although two-thirds of the baby boomers worry about their financial future, the oldest of them claim that they began saving for their retirement in their mid-thirties. The baby-boom generation – the oldest of whom will start to retire officially in the year 2011 – has been raised on the principles of independence and financial security. Their main goals for retirement include good health, financial well-being, and time for the family. Even more than the current generation of elderly, they intend to live as they can and to age in the style to which they have become accustomed.

Many factors influence the type of housing chosen by the elderly. In the same way that people of all ages would prefer to choose the types of homes they live in but are sometimes forced into a different kind, many older people also live in their second or third choice of housing type. The age, health, and income of a person go a long way in determining the type of housing, as well as whether the occupant is an owner or renter, married, widowed, or single. The occupant's own attitude and personal situation are also instrumental: how aware the person is of available services, how willing that person is to make use of them, and what type of support system exists. There are many alternatives to living in an apartment or single-family home in a regular mixed neighbourhood, and it will be useful to review them briefly.

At the opposite end of the housing spectrum from living independently in a home of one's own is the *skilled nursing facility*, commonly known as the nursing home. Sometimes personal choice and independence must be traded for security of health. New stresses on traditional family support structures have also eroded the ability of many to live on their own. One person in a hundred aged from sixty-five to seventy-four lives in a nursing home, as well as one in twenty aged from seventy-five to eighty-four, and one in four over the age of eighty-five. At any one time, experts estimate that about one in five residents of nursing homes need not be there. In actual fact, there is currently a trend away from nursing homes, due to advances in medical science and in-home care. In a recent ten-year period, the over-sixty-five population increased by 18 percent but the number of nursing home residents increased by only 4 percent. Although the number of people over sixty-five is forecast to double by the year 2030, the number of nursing home beds will increase by only two-thirds. Nursing homes are clearly not the growth industry of the future.

There are numerous housing options available to older people, each one tailored to a different level of necessity and care. The choice of housing type should be based on maximizing the safety and health of the occupant, assisting the person to operate at the top of his or her abilities, and creating a home environment which is as comfortable and familiar as possible, with the fewest institutional features. (The dependence upon institutions of all kinds is reflected in the place of death of most people. Regardless of where they choose to live out their final years, almost four out of five people die in a health-care facility; only one in five dies in a private home.)

Especially designed for people over sixty-five, housing known as *independent living apartments* offer the highest level of personal independence short of living on one's own. Apartments of this type are usually found in a highrise building, have one or two bedrooms, and are equipped with a full kitchen. The arrangement differs from a regular apartment block because of the available facilities: a shared dining hall where residents can have one meal a day, a library and exercise room, and a medical team which can respond quickly to emergency calls. *Assisted living apartments* go a step further in accommodating people who need a higher level of care in a home-like environment. Each apartment generally has one bedroom (unless a roommate system is employed) and only a kitchenette since three meals daily are provided. Housekeeping and laundry services are also available, as are resources to assist with daily activities and transportation. The option of assisted living – also known as group housing or shared housing or congregate housing – allows frailer and much older people to retain elements of independence and a sense of dignity while receiving assistance and living with others in similar circumstances.

Only 30 percent of people over the age of sixty-five rent their accommodations. Approximately 5 percent live in nursing homes and 65 percent own their homes. Elderly homeowners can choose their housing type from a variety of options. Retirement communities are one option with many variations. These relatively recent communities originated in the 1920s in Florida when labour and religious groups bought up land with the intention of creating retirement settlements for their members. These communities have experienced real growth and now come in many sizes and categories. *Retirement new towns* are privately developed communities with over five thousand residents. Sun City in Arizona and Leisure World in California are examples of retirement new towns and have populations in the tens of thousands. Many housing forms appear in the same development: single-family detached houses, duplexes, fourplexes, townhouses, both high- and low-rise buildings. The size of these new towns makes it possible for them to have their own medical and emergency services, fire departments and security forces, and numerous businesses including shopping centres, banks, food stores, and restaurants. These towns are intended primarily for healthy and active older people, so they contain many recreational facilities such as swimming pools, golf courses, tennis courts, and lawn bowling greens. Residency in these communities is restricted to people over the age of fifty. The residents tend to be well off because of the high costs involved with the provision of such a wide variety of shared facilities.

*Retirement villages* are smaller versions of retirement new towns, with populations between one thousand and five thousand people. Housing types vary but tend to be uniform within a single village. In some places, mobile homes are the predominant type of housing. Retirement villages generally have communal facilities, but unlike new towns, they are not self-contained communities and usually do not have commercial establishments or health-care services. Arbutus Ridge, on Vancouver Island in British Columbia, is a community of 680 homes of single- and two-storey dwellings, with many on-site amenities including library, health club, games room, and hair salon. Shopping and health services are accessible in a nearby town. *Retirement subdivisions* are smaller yet, with populations not exceeding five hundred, and are built in existing communities. They have a limited array of services since such facilities are available nearby in the larger, adjacent community. Communal facilities are few (perhaps only a meeting room or library). Many of these subdivisions enforce an over-fifty age rule, and the majority of the residents are retirees.

Yet another type of development for the elderly is the *continuing-*

*care retirement community* (CCRC), or the life-care community. This type of living is restricted to the affluent since payment for a CCRC is usually a single lump-sum payment ($100,000 would not be out of the ordinary) plus a high monthly or annual rental fee. Some CCRCs even require a single endowment and then place the resident's assets in the management's care. The life-care community offers health care, medical, religious, legal, even funeral services. The housing is extremely varied within a single development, ranging from independent living in condominiums and cluster housing to nursing-home care. Recreational and social facilities abound, including swimming pools and golf courses, social centres and health spas. CCRCs offer housing with the emphasis on residential rather than institutional, but many residents still find life depressing in these communities. Some experts claim that the elderly find it pleasurable to live with other elderly people, whereas others maintain that old people appreciate the availability of services and facilities but do not like to be reminded constantly that they are old. Many residents of retirement communities feel that all their neighbours, like themselves, will simply fall into ill health and eventually die. Many also do not like the geographical detachment from the locations of the earlier parts of their lives.

Older people who elect not to live in a retirement community or institutional setting and to live instead in a private home in a mixed neighbourhood still have a number of options to choose from. *Home sharing* lets homeowners remain in their familiar accommodations and at the same time provide companionship and additional income for themselves. Fellow home sharers can be people of the same age or younger people who might be willing to undertake some household tasks in exchange for a reduction in rent. An *accessory apartment* gives an older person the opportunity to live in close proximity with younger family members yet maintain a distinct division between households. The accessory apartment is a completely self-contained home built for the purpose into a newly-built house or converted from surplus space in an existing house. The beauty of the concept is that the original house which contains the accessory apartment may belong to the elderly person who moves into the accessory apartment, thereby allowing the other family members to move into the larger unit, or the younger family members may be the owners of the house which contains the accessory apartment to be used by the older relative. A similar idea is the *garden suite* which is a small detached dwelling built on the lot of a larger house. Like the accessory apartment, the garden suite can be built by the older person who then vacates the large home to make way for family members, or it can be built by the family who owns the house and offers the suite to their elderly relative. The garden suite lets older people live close to their families yet still gives them an important measure of independence and privacy. Unfortunately a large number of municipalities have zoning regulations that prevent their construction.

Another method of facilitating independent living for the elderly which also provides a measure of security and family companionship is an arrangement whereby the two households buy *side-by-side or stacked units* in a multi-unit housing structure. For example, if an extended family buys an entire house together, they can make it into a duplex and divide the structure into two units: a ground-floor home for the older family member and an upper unit of two and a half floors for the younger family. At a later date, when the elderly relative dies, the family can either rent out the ground floor, sell it, or reconfigure the house to make it into a single-family unit. The practice of relatives buying neighbouring properties is not a new one, but the idea of designing adjacent housing units that can specifically accommodate this practice is not at all common.

Even if their relatives live nearby, many older people who live in their own homes have need of some form of *in-home help*. Much less expensive than institutionalization, in-home care lets many householders remain in their own homes in a regular mixed-age community. Depending on the level of need, an elderly homeowner or apartment dweller can receive visiting homemaker services that include help with shopping and meal preparation, housework, and personal care. Health-care services are also available for people with chronic conditions or for those who have recently been in the hospital and require follow-up treatment. Transportation services allow older residents to attend appointments and social engagements, and food services (meals-on-wheels) greatly assist people who have trouble with providing their own cooked meals. It is estimated that home care is used by a fifth of older people with the need for such services. Researchers have found that the elderly do not at all mind receiving help with many of the tasks of daily life (such as bathing and cleaning, dressing and eating) so long as they can get about on their own and maintain a social life as long as possible.

An important consideration in designing and modifying homes for the elderly is acknowledging the many physical difficulties experienced by old people in their homes. Accidents are the fifth leading cause of death for people over sixty-five. Many fatal accidents are due to falls which are frequently preventable. Causes of falls include an absence of railings on stairs and of grab bars in the bathroom, uneven surfaces on floors and stairs, inadequate lighting, loose rugs, clutter and mess, and miscalculating the number of stairs. Burns are also a major cause of injuries in the kitchen (stove and oven), bathroom (hot water in the tub and shower), and living room and bedroom (smoking). It is estimated that 3 percent of the elderly live in homes that are severely in need of repair and that 5 percent live in homes with moderate problems.

The major difficulty for older people in their own homes is not primarily the condition of the home or its upkeep but that it has in no way been adapted to their special needs. Features which pose no problem for younger people can be sources of strain and danger for less able people. A proper approach to the modification of housing for the elderly includes a thorough assessment of the needs of the occupants over the course of an extended period of time, followed by implementation of the necessary changes. Edward Steinfeld, in an article entitled "Adapting Housing for Older Disabled People," writes, "Theoretically, physical changes in the dwelling unit should coincide with the user's need for a more supportive environment. The environmental flexibility for accommodating change is worthless unless those options are systematically employed when the resident is in need of them."

The loss of independence due to declining physical capabilities is exacerbated by a host of problems common to many homes of older people. Broken and insufficient furniture, as well as an overabundance of furniture, tangles of electrical wire, and clutter underfoot are typical sources of danger in living rooms. Poor beds (too low, too little support), bad closet design, low temperature, and inadequate lighting are common trouble spots in the bedroom. The kitchen offers numerous difficulties to the older person: a lack of counter space, oven controls behind the stove elements, an oven door that requires bending down, cabinets that are too high to reach. The bathroom is also a mine field, with changes in floor surface, unsecured rugs, problems with getting in and out of the bathtub and on and off the toilet. Many older people change the way they do things – for instance, washing at the sink instead of in the bathtub – rather than change their environments to accommodate the changes they themselves have undergone. A great number of the elderly do not know what to do to make life easier in their homes, or they are hesitant to make changes in the places they live, or they simply lack the money to undertake modifications.

The two areas of the home that most require modification to support independent living by the elderly are the bathroom and the kitchen. Losing the ability to groom and bathe oneself is one of the main reasons older people move into institutions. Difficulties with meal preparations detract from a person's sense of feeling useful and creative and of being in touch with familiar daily activities. All the other areas of the home demand attention as well. The fact that many recommendations can be made nowadays to facilitate aging in place is a sign of the heightened awareness of the topic and of the growth in specialized information on the subject. Options for the elderly used to be simple and few; recent research into aging and housing have yielded numerous methods and preparations for growing old at home. Some basic rules of thumb are offered by Edward Steinfeld when he writes that "adaptations should strive to be unobtrusive, generally useful to all people, dissociated with specific disabilities, and familiar in appearance."

Ideally, a home inhabited by older people should have at least one route that allows the occupants to move from the main entry through to the kitchen, living and dining rooms, bathroom, bedroom, and storage area without having to go up and down any stairs. The related issue of accumulated possessions can be a highly sensitive one.

Most older people have amassed a large quantity of furniture, knick-knacks, and mementoes over the years, and do not take kindly to suggestions by other people that they should suddenly throw out this chair or that box of souvenirs. The fact remains, however, that in the living rooms of many elderly people there is frequently too much furniture, an overflow of clutter, and dangerous tangles of electrical and telephone cords. As far as they are able, older residents should strive to put away much of their stuff into the storage areas of the house rather than leave it about to block pathways and fill the edges of shelves. Actually throwing items out, or recycling them or sending them to charities, are other ways of dealing with a surfeit of possessions. We must emphasize that raising the subject of a person's things is a sensitive topic. An older person must understand the potential danger of tripping over wires and cords, of slipping on loose throw rugs, and of stumbling over piles of magazines stacked on the floor.

A key objective should be to clear the living room of all clutter and mess, and to create a control centre in the room where a person can perform a multitude of functions from a single comfortable chair. This place would preferably be near a window, and from such a chair the person would be able to reach the light switch, the thermostat, the telephone, the remote control for the television, and a small surface for reading material. Since the living room is such a central space in the home, a place used for entertaining and visiting, television watching and music listening, reading and even napping, it is important that its design permits numerous furniture arrangements and space uses. It should be spacious and attractive, with views to the outdoors and an appealing aspect in itself. If possible, the living room should also be able to catch the winter sun in order to inject a little brightness into an otherwise trying season.

The bedroom is another room in the home that should be made as functional and comfortable as possible to accommodate a resident who may have to spend more than just the hours of sleeping in bed. Although the bedrooms of older, bedridden people can benefit from such institutional features as hospital beds (adjustable to many positions, with side rails) and a trapeze device to assist in getting in and out of bed, all bedrooms – regardless of the condition of the resident – need reliable ventilation (but no drafts near the head of the bed), temperature control, lighting, and views to the outdoors. The bed should be positioned in such a way that the person in it has a view out the window. The route to the bathroom must be short and direct.

Using the bathroom can be a trial at the best of times for many elderly people. Even if modifications are not needed when a person is healthy and fit, certain preparations can be made in advance for the time when many of the helpful features will be required or at least appreciated. It is estimated that at least one-third of all bathrooms of people over sixty-five need some changes to make life easier for their users. The door should always open outward for safety, so that the opening won't be blocked in the event that someone falls inside. Non-slip finishes are a must for all floor surfaces. Windows, desirable as they may seem, are not recommended for reasons of privacy and drafts. Many bathroom users of all ages have had the unfortunate experience of hoisting themselves up with the help of a towel rack only to have the fixture come off in their hands. Securely installed grab bars serve an important function when a user gets in or out of the shower or tub and on or off the toilet. Many bars of different materials and colours are available, to avoid an institutional appearance, so an elderly user of the bathroom need not feel that he or she is decrepit simply because the room is outfitted with useful devices.

The issue of lighting in a home affects all rooms in various measures. Older people need more light than younger people, and they have a harder time adjusting their eyes from one level to another. Impaired or weakened vision is best helped by task lighting – that is, illumination directed specifically on the area where the person is reading or eating or preparing dinner. Glare is extremely annoying for older people, and it can be reduced by blinds that are pulled part way down or across a window or by exterior overhangs. Sharp colour contrasts can cause unnecessary distractions and confusion. Light colours reduce high contrast and also contribute to even, balanced lighting. Bright and bold colours can also be used to good effect to identify objects in a room that need to be seen easily, such as door frames and light switches. Contrast can be used on a smaller scale as well, to help differentiate the top of the table from the floor or the handrail from the wall. Certain colours are bad choices for older people: blue and green are sometimes hard to distinguish, so they should not be used in any colour-coding scheme, and dark colours like navy and black should be avoided since they appear dimensionless and opaque to some eyes. Red, orange, and yellow are the easiest to see, but strong shades should not be overdone and are to be reserved for accents or for the end walls of corridors to make the hallway seem shorter and to mark a definitive end to the hall.

Many problems encountered by the elderly at home have to do with the age and condition of their homes. For instance, windows that cannot be opened because of disrepair or that open only with extreme difficulty reduce the sense of control that a person has over the home environment. It is well worth having windows fixed, not only for the desired breezes but for the feeling of independence that comes from living in a home where things work. For doors, problems with gripping are avoided by providing lever handles instead of knobs. If locks are installed on interior doors, they should be the kind that can be opened from the outside.

Stairs can be an immense barrier for older people, both physically and psychologically. Exterior stairs should be avoided unless they are absolutely necessary, as they can be even more dangerous in bad weather and serve as a deterrent to the resident's mobility. Inside stairs are to be installed in the homes of elderly people only between floors; sunken living rooms and the like are a bad idea. A split run of stairs, such as a U-shape with a landing midway, is preferable to a long, straight run. Landings break up the chore of ascending or descending stairs and provide a space for a breather or a refuge in the event of dizziness. Winding stairs are hazardous and should not be a regular feature in the lives of older people. Most accidents on stairs occur as a result of falls on the top or bottom step, due to misjudgment or confusion, so these steps should be painted in a contrasting colour to provide clear definition. A change in texture or a notch in the handrail can also add a tactile cue. Carpets are helpful, to absorb sound and cushion falls. Handrails are essential, on both sides. If stairs are dreaded or even feared by some occupants, they should at least be made as secure and safe as they can be.

Finally, the kitchen. As the room with the greatest number of potential challenges to safe and convenient use by older people, the kitchen works best as a compact, well-designed space with efficient equipment. Centrally located, the kitchen should be directly adjacent to the living and dining areas and ideally should be able to accommodate eating and entertaining as well as other uses such as craft making or even sewing. The kitchen is also a good place to have the laundry facilities. A compact size facilitates an economy of movement, which may imply smaller appliances. Any appliance which can fit in the kitchen and which offers the resident a more comfortable lifestyle is welcome: self-cleaning oven, frost-free refrigerator, blender, toaster oven, jar opener and dishwasher. Although U-shaped kitchens look nice, an L-shape is ideal for an older person since it minimizes the amount of moving around. A continuous work surface that links the fridge, stove and sink permits easy shifting of heavy items along the counter with a reduced risk of burns and spills. A window in the kitchen is a necessity, as is good lighting that does not force people to work in their own shadows. Finishes and walls in light colours reflect the light and produce a nice, evenly lit effect.

The various features on the cabinetry and appliances also deserve close attention. Large, D-shaped handles on drawers and cupboards are recommended for ease of use. Lever faucet handles or a single-arm control is best for the sink, and a double sink benefits those who like to do hand laundering. The oven should have counter space on both sides to make it easier to transfer food. Electric ranges are safer than gas ovens, and controls should be positioned on the front of the appliance rather than at the rear to prevent burns from reaching across a hot stove top. Side-hinged, wall-mounted ovens are preferable to freestanding ovens since less stooping and lifting are involved. Side-by-side fridge/freezers are better than top-bottom arrangements since they allow older people to concentrate their perishable food storage at the level that is most comfortable for them. Any device or installation in the kitchen that promotes safety and comfort, that is affordable, and that can find space is worthy of consideration. Women suffer more accidents at home than men because of their greater involvement in household duties. There really is no good reason for anyone's mother or wife or friend to fall off a chair or stool. Good kitchen design should keep that person on her feet, standing, or on a chair, sitting.

The key to maintaining an independent life in one's own home for as long as possible is to adapt the environment by removing impediments to free movement and to add features which facilitate everyday activity. The benefit of living in a time when so much information on aging is available, and when so many technologies and devices have been developed to assist us with our housing, is that we may partake of these wonderful resources and make our lives easier. The cost can be minimal when compared with the greater expense of moving into various forms of assisted housing. The human cost of leaving home for an institution is very high. The rewards of remaining at home – of successfully aging in place – are immeasurable.

**6**

# Where Exactly Do We Live?

M ost people have opinions about which buildings or public spaces they like or dislike, although, if questioned on their taste, they may be hard pressed to give hard reasons for their preferences. Even if only at a subconscious level, people are generally aware of the numerous components which make up their built environment, of the design elements which form the houses and towers and streets which surround them. Everyone responds in some manner to the shapes and lines, the forms and figures, the spaces and absences that comprise their urban, suburban, or rural landscapes. Natural objects very easily occupy our senses of perception: a mountain shaped like a triangle looms in the distance, a tall tree with a circular canopy fills the end of the street, a border of red flowers lines the sidewalk. Buildings and paved surfaces – which actually make up more of the city dweller's environment than natural objects – are frequently overlooked. But the design of our cities and living spaces (whether we care to acknowledge it or not) is a vital aspect of our civic lives. The design of our built environments can make us feel secure and stimulated, or it can frustrate and alienate us. The balance of objects within our view – the harmony of their proportions – is important not only in an aesthetic sense but also in a social and personal way. The effect on a person of living in an ugly environment can be debilitating, just as living in beautiful surroundings can be uplifting.

In the years since the end of the Second World War the aesthetic element in the design of a comfortable environment has been neglected in favour of functional efficiency. We live in a mechanical and technological age. To speak of harmony, balance, and a sense of scale in keeping with human proportions – concepts which have been vital components of architecture and civic design since ancient times – is to court ridicule and laughter in the fast-paced, cut-throat world of deadlines, profit, and achievement. New developments and cities are built to be strong and impressive, large and efficient. Big is good, bigger is better, huge is best. City squares are vast, streets are wide enough to accommodate wave upon wave of rush-hour traffic, new buildings are tall and lean but isolated and out of context with their fellows. Outdoor spaces are designed and buildings are constructed without much consideration for historical continuity. Human scale as a measure of our built environment is absent. No wonder people feel tiny and inconsequential within their new urban landscapes. No wonder so many city dwellers feel a vague sense of unease when pressed to comment on their attitude towards the overall appearance of suburbia.

Andres Duany, an architect who is an adherent of New Urbanism in design – of a return to the traditional principles of city planning and residential design which used to make our built environments so appealing and easy to live with – has commented that an urban pattern which existed in North America for over two hundred years was broken in the years following the Second World War. In a traditional town, small buildings lined the streets and larger civic buildings surrounded rectangular spaces, creating pleasant places to live. A number of reasons have been advanced to account for the degradation of these traditional ideals of building and designing: the rise of specialized industrialization, the rapid increase in population and the resulting appetite for more housing at whatever cost, and the effect of Modernism in architecture, with its aversion to most traditional principles. Suburban sprawl has heavily damaged the balance of our cities, divorcing environmental context from design and removing the concept of scale from the creation of neighbourhoods.

Many people value the wide-open spaces of suburbia, considering it to be a mark of success in life that they have escaped the noise and congestion of city life in exchange for the quiet and expansiveness of the suburbs. One way of gauging the sense of dislocation that can be experienced at the edge of our cities is to observe the reaction of a foreign-born person who is put down in the middle of a suburban street and asked to find his way. "Why are the houses on either side of the street so far away from one another?" the person will ask. "Why are the front yards so big? Why are the streets so wide and empty? Where is the grocery store? The bakery? Where, in fact, are all the people who supposedly live out here?"

Academics and architectural writers are in agreement that city streets are successful when they create a sense of enclosure. Most people feel safe and secure when buildings facing one another are relatively close and when they form the appearance of an enclosing wall. Some theoreticians have assigned numbers to varying degrees of scale and have devised a ratio to account for the relationship between an observer at street level and the object (building or house) under observation. This ratio expresses the height of a building relative to the distance which separates it from the building across the road. According to this system, a height-to-distance ratio of one-to-one (a building at the same height as the distance from the building facing it) presents an object which is part of a larger whole (that is, the rest of the block) and whose details are easily discernible. At a ratio of one-to-two (the height of a house is half the distance from the opposite house), the observed object is perceived as separate and unique. At one-to-three the object still dominates the view, but at one-to-four it blends in with its surroundings. A one-to-one ratio is considered suitable for neighbourhood streets, where pedestrians are the main users. A ratio of one-to-one-and-a-half is appropriate for streets shared equally by cars and pedestrians. Typical Parisian streets have this proportion. When the ratio hits one-to-two or more, the street in question should be a main city street, one used more by cars than pedestrians. As an indication of how the suburbs have departed from all sense of habitable scale, most suburbs have height-to-distance ratios ranging from one-to-six to one-to-ten.

The hunger for ever greater amounts of living space is evidenced in the escalating quantity of land used by each person in the United States. In the two decades following the Second World War average space usage doubled, from one-fifth of an acre of urban land per resident in 1950 to two-fifths in 1970. Such an increase was to be expected given the preference of families with dependent children for detached single-family houses. More compact, higher-density forms of housing are, not surprisingly, far less expensive. The cost of sewers and roads for homes which are closer together is lower than for detached houses spread out over the landscape, and the energy bills are not as high for homes which share walls with their neighbours. The greatest impediment to building smaller and more affordably is the aura of suspicion attached to the very terms "high density" and "compact" which are mistakenly taken as euphemisms for "jammed together" and "tiny," not to mention the negative associations with "low-cost housing" and even "affordable housing." A large house with a spacious lawn on all sides may be attractive and attainable for some, but for many people this type of home is unaffordable, unnecessary, and undesirable.

The expansion of cities outward is a phenomenon that cannot continue at a ravenous pace for much longer. Open fields, woods, and prime farmland are gobbled up on the periphery of cities (two million acres of farmland are developed annually), while the abandoned urban core deteriorates further. The demand for additional single-family houses in the suburbs is an assumption that is increasingly questioned: with smaller households and fading confidence in the ability to undertake a long-term financial commitment such as a mortgage on an expensive house, do we really need more big-ticket homes? Would it not be both efficient and prudent to provide smaller homes in smaller-scale, sustainable communities?

The consideration of quality of life is also an issue. James Garbarino addresses the sparseness of suburbia in his essay on the ecological perspective of housing for children in his book *Habitats for Children*. He differentiates between the original suburbs, which were small towns at the edges of cities with railway commuting stations as their focus, and newer suburbs, which are bedroom communities almost entirely dependent on automobile transportation. "The new suburbs," he writes, "seem to add little to a family's personal resources for child rearing and may in fact detract, because they lack enough community activities (formal and informal) to offer children a socially rich and varied existence. Those 'post-industrial' suburbs are technology intensive and often socially deficient." Garbarino supports strong urban neighbourhoods which have all the opportunities of big cities together with the social qualities of small towns. A weak neighbourhood – like many in the sprawling suburbs – has so few resources, he argues, that "it impoverishes the social experience and knowledge of children."

Sociologists and economists have pointed out that the best places to live – the places with the highest levels of civic welfare – are not neighbourhoods with the highest property values or areas where the lots are the largest, but cities and towns in which small and medium-sized businesses flourish. Communities maintain long-term population growth and economic health when people are tied to the community and when they change house infrequently. These communities share a number of characteristics, including the presence of locally-owned manufacturing firms which invest in the community, thriving volunteer associations, many places of worship with strong attendance, a variety of small retail establishments (bars, restaurants, cafés, grocery stores and the like), a high percentage of family households with children, and high levels of homeownership. Clearly, a neighbourhood can be designated as good not because its members live in large houses with sprawling yards but because it contains businesses and residents actively involved in the social and economic life of the community.

Suburbs, in themselves, are not essentially bad. The land is cheaper on the fringe of cities. Industry and jobs have been relocating away from the city centre for decades. The operative word is "sprawl." Land adjacent to cities is not limitless and it should not be wasted. Large developments of big houses are no longer the primary need in housing. Whether downtown or in a suburb, the answer to the greatest demand in housing, both socially and economically, may just be a well-designed but flexible compact home in a dense and varied environment. No one wants to live in a crime-ridden highrise hell, ignored by municipal politicians, developers, and home buyers. At the other end of the scale, there must be an alternative to living in a setting where you must drive to the mall to pick up a quart of milk. Somewhere in between lies the type of neighbourhood most of us have seen and admired for its charm and friendliness: shops and services within easy walking distance, variety in the appearance and size of the buildings, frequent squares and parks, accessible public transit, people sitting on porches, neighbours chatting, children playing outdoors. Such a neighbourhood need not be a showcase for expensive townhouses, or unsafe, or in Europe. With proper planning and design neighbourhoods like these (built new *and* affordably) can be a North American reality.

Apprehensions with regard to smaller-scale housing are common, but most of them boil down to prejudices and irrational fears. In a residential area composed only of detached houses, there is an average of five to seven homes per acre. Rowhouses can be built at a density varying from seventeen to thirty-two homes per acre, depending on the width of the house and on whether there are driveways and back alleys. That makes three to six times as many rowhouses in a given piece of land compared with detached houses. Does this mean that rowhouses are a crowded form of housing, unsuited to families? Certainly not. Do higher-density developments at an urban scale in the city centre or in the suburbs create neighbourhoods destined to be crowded, crime-ridden and nasty? Again, no.

Bad neighbourhoods are characterized by poor neighbourly relations, inadequate contact between children, insufficient housing, elevated levels of stress, deficient social support systems, and an overall feeling of resignation, deprivation, and negativity. The creation of new homes which are compact, well-designed, affordable to a wide range of the home-buying public, and planned to fit in with existing city neighbourhoods or to mirror a comfortable urban scale even at the edge of a large city does not necessarily lead to substandard home life. Just the opposite, in fact. A smart new neighbourhood accessible to a greater chunk of the population than only those who can afford an expensive house is appealing both to people with a limited budget and to those who deliberately choose a home which will not suck out every last penny of their available cash. If we are searching for an alternative to five homes per acre, that alternative will have to be attractive to as many people as possible.

One unavoidable but contentious contributing factor to the increasing consumption of land by the suburbs is the prevalence of the automobile. It is difficult to ascertain which is the cause of the other: the car which enabled access to the far-flung neighbourhoods at the edge of cities, or the suburb which demanded car ownership of its inhabitants as a precondition of residence. A hundred years ago there was one car for every ten thousand people; in 1940 there was one car per five people; and now there is one car for every second person. In 1960, only one in five households had two or more cars; today, three in five are two-car households. All of these vehicles produce pollution; in fact, motor vehicles are the source of more than half of all hazardous air pollutants. Driving only twenty-five miles dumps a pound of pollutants into the air, all of which can cause smog and acid rain, breathing problems, reduced lung function, asthma, bronchitis, eye and nose irritation, lowered resistance to colds and other infections, not to mention the damage to plants and trees and to the stone in cities, causing erosion to historic buildings, monuments, and statues. Whether new or old, motor vehicles swarm over the continent, spewing their emissions and gobbling up land for expressways and roads – a total of almost four million miles at last count.

The car is an undeniable reality, and to argue against its existence would be pointless. Its effect on all our lives has been immeasurable. Rather than ride on public transportation, many people drive. Children used to walk to school, but now they are driven, sometimes while still eating their breakfast. People used to walk to their houses of worship, but most now take the car. Many more people drive to work than all those combined who take the bus or walk. As a general statistic, each person travels an average of twenty-eight miles per day, mostly by car, an increase of over two miles in only ten years, and every household takes an average of five trips daily, an increase of one trip over the past thirty years. Many of our public institutions are constructed like islands in a sea of concrete and asphalt, with buildings surrounded by a parking lot where visitors and shoppers can leave their cars. New forms of motor vehicle have been created to suit the perceived wishes of suburbanites and of urban would-be adventurers: the minivan, to fit children, pets and carpoolers, and the sport utility vehicle for those whose tastes do not run to family sedans and minivans. Of course, roads have expanded to accommodate all these vehicles. Over the decades, roads have been built ever wider. Buildings and houses drift farther apart, the intervening spaces filled with motorists idling in traffic, pulling in and out of their driveways, speeding along highways, and negotiating the everyday perils of city streets.

In the not-too-distant past, streets were built to a human scale. Back lanes provided access to the rear of homes. Setbacks were not mandated by zoning bylaws, so buildings came right up to and defined the edge of the pavements comprising sidewalk and street. In the late nineteenth and early twentieth centuries, various design and planning movements influenced the way some cities laid out their streets and zoned their residential areas. The City Beautiful movement called for a sense of order and for greater access of all citizens to sunlight and fresh air. Cities responded with setback bylaws whereby buildings had to be constructed at a minimum distance from the public sidewalk. The thinking ran that the existence of front yards would not only provide more sunlight and fresh air but would also encourage the planting of trees and other vegetation. The Garden City movement promoted country-style living, with plenty of public green space to offer salubrious living conditions for the inhabitants. Setbacks in new neighbourhoods in park-like surroundings were extended to 15 and 20 feet. The increasing numbers of automobiles led to the creation of new street widths to handle the traffic and parking requirements: residential streets almost 70 feet wide, commercial streets 80 feet. The wider roads, together with the deeper setbacks, resulted in streets with height-to-distance ratios of up to one-to-six. The relationship between building and street was lost. The definition of the street edge was also lost. Human scale as an essential component of civic design was gone.

The suburbs built after the Second World War were subject to many zoning bylaws that regulated the width of streets, the height of buildings, the size of houses, the type of façade a home in a certain neighbourhood could have, land use (residential, commercial, or industrial), and density. Residential roads were built inordinately wide and intersections were designed to accommodate the largest possible turning radius for a car. Low-rise apartment buildings were built far back on their lots, commercial buildings even farther to provide ample parking for clients and shoppers. The combined effect of all this widening and distancing was to shrink the pedestrian, to make the person at street level feel tiny and far away from the buildings intended to provide service and shelter. The type of suburban residential development made up of thousands of look-alike houses on short winding streets exacerbated the situation: the human being as ant.

The involvement of North Americans with streets and cars is directly linked to housing through that part of the home which is specifically designed for motor vehicles – the garage. Over a half of all households have a garage or carport incorporated into their homes. Over three-quarters of all detached single-family houses have a garage with space for two or more cars, up from just over a half in the mid-1970s. Garages are deemed an essential component of the home, no less important than the bathroom or kitchen. Some larger homes are so inelegantly designed that the multiple garage doors facing the street and taking up such a huge proportion of the façade make the place look like a do-it-yourself carwash, the kind with numerous self-serve bays. The irony is that the garage is often used for storage of everything but cars. A great number of people who have garages will confess, perhaps with some embarrassment, that they park one or more of their cars in the driveway or on the street because there is no room in the garage. There are newly-built suburban houses that deal with the problem of excess storage material and car shelter by providing garages for three cars. A typical three-car garage takes up 900 square feet of space, roughly the same size as the average home built in the 1950s.

Too many people think immediately of foreign lands when presented with the image of homes and streets built to a comfortable, human scale. "The cute little houses were packed in cheek by jowl," the animated tourist might say upon return from a trip to Italy,

Greece, the south of France. "The narrow, winding streets had such charm and character," the same tourist might report. "People sit at tables on the sidewalks in front of cafés to have their morning coffee." Civic buildings positioned around a central square, weekly outdoor markets, numerous restaurants filled with townsfolk at lunch, small shops selling housewares and handicrafts and jewelry, attractive homes with character and individual identity, a sense of history: these are characteristics of exotic tourist destinations in far-off places such as Provence or Corfu, the city-dwelling North American will claim. And what exactly do we find in our own cities? Must our inner cities be corrupt versions of what for many is a foreign fantasy?

Let us consider a worst-case scenario, a neighbourhood in decline in a large city on the eastern seaboard – Charles Village in Baltimore, Maryland. The neighbourhood is about a hundred city blocks in size, adjacent to a major hospital campus, museum, and stadium, and home to roughly fifteen thousand people. Originally constructed in the latter decades of the nineteenth century as upscale housing outside the urban core, it once served as a transition zone from city to country. The brick Victorian townhouses, adorned generously with bay windows, balconies, and gables, used to be home to upper-middle-class citizens who moved out years ago to more recent suburbs, and the grand old houses have since been subdivided into tiny rental units. The city organizes panels and committees and devises master plans to rejuvenate the neighbourhood, but in the meantime the area is beset with many problems: crime (drugs, theft, vandalism), sanitation (indiscriminate dumping, rats), neglect (absentee landlords, lack of building maintenance), and stalled development (empty lots, vacant buildings). Services such as grocery and hardware stores are lacking even though there is no shortage of liquor shops and pizza joints. Most people rent their homes. Who would go to the trouble of buying and renovating in such a place? All the elements for a fine neighbourhood are there – solid houses, a suitable urban scale, proximity to downtown – but the area has been ignored by the homeowning crowd, abandoned in favour of an alternative version of city living, of a suburban lifestyle where things are safer, cleaner, and more wholesome.

A similar situation exists in the city centre of Winnipeg, Manitoba. With a population of over six hundred thousand people, Winnipeg used to be the third largest city in Canada, but it is now ranked eighth. The fourteen neighbourhoods designated as "major improvement areas" by the city's community services department are all in the core area or directly adjacent. Whereas the average price of a residential home in Winnipeg rose by 5 percent over a recent ten-year period, the values of the houses in the fourteen depressed neighbourhoods declined by almost 50 percent (to an average of just over $23,000 in 1999). The unemployment rate in these neighbourhoods is four times the city average. The crime rates are five times higher than the rest of the city. Over the years, the businesses on the downtown streets have closed and moved to the outlying areas where new housing developments and malls have been built. People who live outside the core area rarely venture downtown to shop, and most would never consider living or owning property there. They might bemoan the decline in the fortunes of their downtown – many older residents remember a friendly and vibrant central Winnipeg – but they choose to spend their time and money elsewhere.

What of life in the smaller cities and towns? Let us now consider two towns in the Midwest, one thriving, the other struggling. The first is Wilmington, Ohio, a farming community of ten thousand residents, the better part of an hour from the nearest big city. Most of the housing is single-family detached with clapboard exterior. People wave from cars, say hello on the street. Two decades ago, a major shipping company relocated its headquarters to this town. Many new jobs were created and other businesses were attracted to the area. People from nearby cities moved to the town to benefit from the slower pace and the cheaper cost of living (although they soon found that the special friendliness they had observed amongst the townsfolk was not extended to them – newcomers were considered to be different from the long-time residents). With the arrival of the shipping company, the commercial focus shifted from the downtown area to a strip near the big plant at the edge of town. The street is lined with fast-food restaurants, discount emporiums, and big-box superstores. The downtown core has become less busy and a touch shabby, but the town is considered a success because it has a good employment rate and because it is growing.

The other town, Clay Center, Kansas, is a struggling town, which also has its roots in farming and is home to five thousand citizens. The population has been dropping for decades. Two new malls have opened outside of town, in opposite directions, and they have drained shoppers from the stores on the town's main street. The bus service along the two-lane highway leading in and out of town was cancelled a few years back, leaving many of the businesses without daily deliveries of goods and parts. The town has not been able to attract any new manufacturing companies or high-tech industries. The spirit of deregulation has swept through the countryside, ending the subsidization of commerce and transportation. Not many of the town's teenagers intend to stay around after graduation – they are all planning lives in cities and suburbs. We must acknowledge that the cities (those same cities which have wastelands at their centres) control the fate of smaller towns, sending out businesses and jobs or taking them away, in both cases casting a blight on the downtown areas of these places.

Finally, a peculiarity of a postwar suburban community on the west coast, in Irvine, California. If we are to provide brief profiles of life in the city and life in the town, we cannot omit certain oddities of life in the suburbs. This municipality, developed in the 1960s, is home to over one hundred thousand people and is situated fifty-odd miles from Los Angeles. The residential part is in the centre and the commercial and industrial facilities are on the fringes. The majority of the homes are single-family detached houses. In some areas, street after street of similar houses in the same colour and style are grouped into neighbourhoods with their own shopping mall, swimming pool, and recreation centre. The look of the houses cannot change, no matter what the tastes or preferences of the owners: deed restrictions forbid customization by the homeowners. This is, in fact, an almost farcical version of the typical suburb. Here the houses are destined to look identical for ever.

Zoning is the mechanism that regulates how communities (including, of course, the suburbs) are built and maintained. Zoning bylaws are devised with some input from urban planners and are passed by elected municipal officials who represent the citizenry. These bylaws determine not only street width and building height but minimum lot coverage (a house must take up a certain minimal area on a lot) and land use (whether or not, for instance, a certain neighbourhood can have grocery stores at the street corners). Zoning serves to maintain established values, to ensure that homeowners do not lose on their housing investments by the sudden introduction of changes to the neighbourhood.

Zoning preserves the status quo. If a suburb was built in the post-war years, for example, and it represented a particular demographic distribution unique to the time, zoning bylaws prevent any sizable modifications to the neighbourhood even if the overall composition of society has significantly changed and the existing homes no longer satisfy the needs of the new home-buying public. In other words, if a suburb was built entirely of large houses for families with three or four children each, and those children have now grown up and left an elderly couple with a home that is too large for their needs, there is no way the older parents can subdivide their house and rent out half of it as a separate housing unit. In this respect, zoning frequently operates to exclude a great number of potential homeowners from certain neighbourhoods. It functions to keep the area from adapting to changes in social make-up and it rarely accommodates the current demographic diversity. Zoning does not allow mixed-use and mixed-type neighbourhoods. If a series of streets was designed not to have a mix of modest and expensive homes or corner stores, then that is the way the neighbourhood will remain.

Today's suburbs and the homes in them do not represent the ongoing shift in demographics. The developers who have built these homes had them designed for traditional families and not for the multi-faceted array of current potential homeowners. The suburbs make for fine neighbourhoods for the people who live in them, whose obvious interest is to maintain their property values and to protect them from deterioration, but they exclude too many of the people who are simply looking for homes to buy. Suburbs, in this respect, are segregated areas: by income and also by race. The notion of mixing subpopulations is foreign to the culture of suburbia. But the economy has changed and our social composition has changed. Seen from a hard and practical viewpoint, the preservation of sprawling areas of habitable land for a shrinking segment of the population makes no real sense at all.

No one is calling for the demolition of the suburbs or for the displacement of its inhabitants. What would make sense, however, is the realignment of priorities and objectives when it comes to planning and zoning suburban neighbourhoods. New building should create streets and homes with higher densities which mirror a comfortable, urban, human scale. Communities with a proven balance of easily accessible small businesses and of homes in all shapes, sizes, and prices to suit the widest clientele should be allowed to co-exist and thrive. When it comes to homes already in place, it would not undermine the principles of homeownership, open commerce, and fair play to alter zoning to allow the introduction of new uses for existing structures, such as parts of houses used as home businesses, garden suites, and the division of large homes into two separate units. If times have changed – and indeed they have – we must reassess our way of using land and buildings for housing the citizenry. Current bylaws and regulations should be loosened to permit methods of housing that properly reflect the financial and social conditions of the population.

The primary purpose of housing, needless to say, is to provide homes for people. A collection of homes makes up a neighbourhood, and it is hoped that the two together – homes and neighbourhood – create a sense of community. Everyone lives in a neighbourhood of some sort, but not everyone can claim to live in a community. Many people (both apartment dwellers and homeowners) will readily admit that they do not know their neighbours, that they never bump into anyone they know in the shops and streets that surround their homes, that they never wave or nod hello to other people as they get out of the car, stroll along the street, or wait in line at the cash register. Communities are formed through a series of physical opportunities. Actual places in the neighbourhood create the settings for these opportunities. Public swimming pools, pedestrian walkways with benches, parks and playgrounds, and bustling streets with many shops and services are locations and facilities in the public realm that provide the opportunities for parents to play with children and to meet other parents and children, for retired folk to encounter their friends, for young people to get together and hang out.

Opportunity-creating places bring people closer together. Many such places have disappeared from housing developments in the past few years in the name of land use efficiency, crime prevention, and a developer's sense of what makes a neighbourhood appealing. Homes and developments are designed so that front yards are empty expanses of lawn that distance people from street activity, confining all life to the indoors or the backyard. Houses are spaced wide apart with little opportunity for neighbours to bump into one another on a casual basis. Active shopping streets are missing, replaced by the new social and commercial opportunity of the postwar era: the shopping mall.

Malls have taken the place of Main Street in North America. In the first two decades following the Second World War when shopping centres sprouted across the land, suburbanites followed a recognizable pattern of shopping behaviour; they abandoned the stores in their own city centres or on the streets of neighbouring towns and travelled very little outside their own suburb to do their shopping. In the decades that followed, the devastating effect of the malls was reflected in the changing face of downtown streets. Malls in both the suburbs and in the city centre drew away the shoppers from the sidewalks and led them to indoor, glassed-atrium environments.

Once-profitable stores on once-busy streets were forced to shut down or move to a mall, reducing even further the number of pedestrians on the pavements. The city centre was gradually emptied, leaving behind vacant storefronts which were snapped up as strip clubs, sex shops, pizza joints – hardly the stuff of a thriving downtown economy.

The effect of the big-box superstores is similar. Whenever a monster discount store opens at the edge of a city or in a mall, the smaller discount shops in town are the first to go, finding it impossible to compete with the selection and prices on offer in the huge chain store. Next to be killed off are the regular shops downtown – the small places that sell fabrics and shoes, sports equipment and stationery. Hardware outlets are frequent casualties, as are grocery stores who have their market for cleaning supplies and canned goods whisked away. Even service companies decline when the hypermart comes to town; people increasingly find that it is easier and cheaper to buy inexpensive new appliances than to have their broken items repaired.

Malls come in all sizes. The typical suburban mall can have about half a million square feet of leasable space, a couple of department stores to anchor the complex, and parking for three thousand cars. The largest mall in the United States, Mall of America in Bloomington, Minnesota, has over four million square feet, four hundred shops, four department stores, and an amusement park. The largest in Canada (and in the world), West Edmonton Mall in Alberta, has over eight hundred stores and services, dozens of cinemas, a water park and ice arena, dolphin shows, and a casino. Designers and operators of malls have as their objective the creation of an environment which will attract the maximum number of shoppers and be conducive to the greatest expenditure by those shoppers. Layout and signage are employed to move people to all corners of the mall, to make them pass by as many stores as possible, and to trigger impulsive shopping behaviour. Bumping into someone in a mall is more like an interruption or a temporary distraction than an opportunity to chat or catch up on news and gossip. The experience of shopping on Main Street – natural lighting, street sounds, restaurants and cafés, neighbourhood familiarity – is replaced in the mall by muzak, splashing fountains, the press of crowds, and food courts. The simple green park as an open space in the middle of the city is replaced by the mall parking lot.

Picture a certain scene from a mall: an older person, alone on a bench, hat in lap, styrofoam cup of coffee in hand, too pooped to go into one more store or follow around younger family members. What goes through this person's mind? What memories? Perhaps a vision of a city or town that no longer exists, of outdoor streets filled with shoppers, stores both big and small, fresh air. A balance of street life and home life: sitting on the porch, reading the newspaper and watching neighbourhood kids on bikes, then getting up to walk to the store at the end of the block. That walk would be part of a daily routine, an agreeable task. It might be a long walk or a short one, the kind where you just throw on a jacket and leave the house. No car keys, no battling traffic, no endless circling in the lot to find a spot. The walk might even be shorter than the distance from the parked car to the doors of the shopping mall.

7

# Home as a Consumer Product

"**B**uying a house is the biggest investment that most people will ever make in their lives." This statement is easily one of the most common made with regard to homeownership, particularly for first-time owners. Without doubt, buying a home is a very serious transaction. When you commit yourself to paying off a mortgage over the course of some twenty-five years, you make a decision with long-term implications that will influence all of your other important decisions. You will have to work harder, worry more about keeping your job, perhaps even change your lifestyle now that you have signed on the dotted line at the bank. On the basis of this huge commitment, you will have to make compromises that affect everything from buying new clothes to choosing a college for the children. A home is definitely a major purchase, arguably the largest in anyone's life. But an *investment*? Why don't people say that buying a house is the biggest *purchase* that they will ever make? An investment implies carefully committing a goodly sum of money in the expectation of earning a profit. Profit is what most people hope to gain when they make an investment. But since when have people come to expect that they can buy a product (in this case a home), use it intensively, and then sell it after a number of years and *still* make a profit? Homes have somehow become a commodity, an article of commerce to be included in an investment portfolio and then traded at just the right moment for maximum profit. The consumerism which has become so much a part of our regular daily lives has even taken over the way we think of such basic concepts as domesticity.

People rank home as the item in their lives which says the most about themselves – ahead of their jobs, hobbies, vacation destinations, or any of their personal possessions. Over three-quarters of the citizens of the United States claim that owning a home is a major part of the American Dream, an increase of 8 percent over a recent five-year period. Yet the attachment to home appears to be more an attachment to the *concept* of home than to the actual home itself. How else can one explain the huge internal migration of North Americans? One person in six changes house every year. On average, every person moves about a dozen times per lifetime. One-third of all renters and one-tenth of all homeowners move each year. It is difficult to imagine that the stress and sense of discontinuity and expense created by moving house on such a national scale can be undertaken without the expectation of financial gain. No people with a strong attachment to land and location would be capable of such restlessness. Joel Garreau, in *Edge City: Life on the New Frontier*, writes:

> Homes have become financial commodities more than emotional entities … [H]omes became people's prime savings repository: their retirement nest egg, kids' inheritance, college savings plan,

ticket to a European vacation. Christmas memories in the living room were no longer vital. Nor could doorjambs be treasured for recording the height of children as they grew. Nor could these homes be secure havens for succeeding generations. For what was important was how easily and efficiently these places – these financial instruments – could be turned over when the time came to cash in and move on. Any feelings of community they represented were held hostage to the ever-present need to trade up. Americans think nothing of moving. Families get larger, they move. Families get smaller, they move. Go to college, get a job, get married, get divorced, get remarried, get promoted, retire – each time, they move. Americans will leave behind houses that were the most emotion-filled places of their lives to move to a "retirement community."

Compared with countries where societies have settled in the same locations for many generations, where cities have existed for hundreds of years, the United States and Canada are relatively recent developments, nations of immigrants and adventurers. In places where houses are centuries old, homes are passed on within families. Sometimes these homes are lost through calamity and natural disaster, war or loss of fortune. But the attitude towards a home that has been owned by a particular family for a long time is one of respect and permanence. The building is maintained and restored with the passage of years. Continuity is essential: of appearance, of its position within the community, of ownership. How many North Americans have had a house in their family for generations? How many people who live in a house over one hundred years old know exactly when it was constructed, who its builder and designer were? Do owners of older homes have any clue as to the history of the house's renovations? Have alterations over the years reflected the lives and interests of the inhabitants and have these changes been made with respect and aesthetic integrity? On the whole, such questions are difficult to answer on this continent. In fact, they are generally irrelevant to most people, inapplicable to the experience of the majority of homeowners.

North America is a place where the inhabitants pack up and move when opportunities seem to be brighter and more promising elsewhere. During the California Gold Rush in the middle of the nineteenth century, for instance, the population of the state grew by many hundreds of thousands per decade, increasing fivefold overall in the four decades leading up to the year 1900. Over the next fifty years the number of people in California leapt from one and a half million to over ten million. Today there are over thirty million residents in the state, as many as in Canada as a whole. People not only race from one coast to another in search of a better life but they have been steadily migrating from the country to the city since the turn of the century. In 1900 only two-fifths of the population was urban; today city folk outnumber country folk by three to one.

The desire to leave squalid and cramped living conditions is another potent stimulus for switching one home for another. The New York City tenements of the later decades of the nineteenth century, for example, housed many of the immigrants who flowed into America at the time. Four times as long as they were wide, each tenement flat was frequently home to more than one family. Lighting and ventilation were inadequate, and until 1879 these flats were not required to have more than a single window in the front or rear. After this date, central shafts provided some additional light and air, although they were just as often used for trash disposal. Toilets were located in the cellars only. Disease and crime were widespread. No person who lived in such housing – or who lives in inadequate conditions at the present time – could be faulted for looking for a way out. It is unreasonable to expect anyone to remain willingly in a home that lacks space and is poorly kept up and is, in general, ugly and mean.

Many homeowners decide to cling to the houses they bought decades ago rather than thrust themselves into the realm of the unknown and the unfamiliar. Owners of bungalows measuring well under 1,000 square feet and built during the Second World War, for instance, have made numerous changes to their small homes over the years to make them more livable. These changes will doubtless increase the monetary value of the property, but most renovations were undertaken to improve the quality of life within the home. Old coal sheds were extended and converted into usable living space, kitchens modified to include laundry facilities (some of these houses lack basements), storage shelves built into wall cavities, and old out-buildings turned into offices. Many of the owners of such homes have chosen to remain in them for more than sentimental reasons. In many cases, the financial wherewithal to trade up was not present. But rather than sniff around for another home, a home which might presumably be "better," the longtime owners of wartime homes improved their houses to make them more useful and spacious, for reasons of efficiency, beautification, and pride. Increasing resale value was certainly not a motivating consideration.

The desire for an additional home is more strong at present than ever before. A vacation home is surely a pleasant thing, a luxury for some, a regular fact of life for others. But its current popularity is an indication of the commodification of our housing, of the yearning for a piece of real estate as proof of social standing. Owning a vacation home is the number-one status symbol of adults: seven in ten people agree that a vacation home is a sign of achievement in life, and six in ten claim they would like to own a vacation home more than anything else. At the beginning of the 1990s eight in ten people said that being the top executive in a large corporation was the primary status symbol. Back then, owning a vacation home was way down on the list (number ten), trailing behind living in an important neighbourhood or having a key position in government. We can assume that there has been no huge upsurge in the basic desire for a rustic getaway or cottage: the change has come in the form of a shift in values. Owning a certain kind of home and having the good fortune to own a second home have become acknowledged signs of acquisition and achievement.

Understandably, the professional builders of homes have always been in the business of providing housing with the expectation of earning a profit for themselves. Whether they build a grand home for a single client with the help and input of an architect or develop a neighbourhood of hundreds of homes using their own in-house designers, their objective is to offer a desirable product at a price that makes the whole enterprise attractive to both the builder and the buyer of the home. The mass production of housing in the immediate postwar years was the beginning of a new era in the provision of homes, when single firms could pump hundreds of units onto the market. The builder William Levitt created a community of over seventeen thousand homes on Long Island, New York, during the years from 1946 to 1951, an achievement made possible by large-scale purchasing of materials, economical and efficient use of land, extensive use of prefabricated components, and a production style which relied heavily on labour specialization and assembly-line techniques. He produced two styles of homes, Cape Cod and Ranch House, at a unit cost of $7,900, in the first year after the Second World War. At the peak of their production, Levitt & Sons put up one 800-square-foot home every fifteen minutes.

Encouraged by a new housing act in 1949 which promoted the development of even greater numbers of homes and by restrictive FHA covenants which ensured neighbourhood homogeneity and conformity, Levitt went on to create other mass-produced, single-family communities: in Pennsylvania in the early 1950s and in New Jersey in the latter half of the decade. Before the war, developers would purchase tracts of land, service them, and sell them off in parcels to buyers or small builders who then hired architects. The legislation of 1949 made it profitable for the developers to build the houses as well. The result was suburban communities of identical homes, preplanned neighbourhoods of look-alike, low-cost, detached houses. The mass-produced housing was extremely attractive to returning war veterans who could obtain thirty-year mortgages without downpayments and with low monthly costs.

The development of instant suburban communities in the postwar period shifted the emphasis from innovation in housing design to innovation in marketing strategy. Mass-produced homes were less expensive than architect-designed homes, and their builders relied on features which would make the small houses appear more attractive and prestigious. Homebuyers were lured by offers of shopping centres, playgrounds, and public swimming pools included as part of the suburban package. Economies of scale did not preclude the provision of carports, storage space in unfinished attics, tiled bathroom walls, and built-in bookcases beside the fireplace. A huge segment of the population needed affordable homes and the government had established guidelines and limits for assisted housing. Canny builders and developers eagerly adapted to the situation and grew wealthy by constructing new complexes of curving roads and uniform houses. Much of this building activity was later criticized for the uninspiring sameness of its appearance and for its tendency to target a particular buyer (middle class, traditional family, white) to the exclusion of other household types. This new style of housing provision – whether praised because it transformed numerous citizens into proud homeowners or damned because it created the type of suburb that people love to hate – also initiated a new style of marketing: the presentation of house as economical purchase, home as a good buy.

Builders quickly learned how to make homes look more appealing. Plate-glass windows made a house look more spacious. A fireplace with a chimney projecting from the side of the house imparted a sense of power to the home (even though the fireplace was not functional as a source of heat). Masonry on the facade gave the impression of permanence, and dormers added a traditional touch. Builders figured out which models the public liked and built them, taking into account regional variations in taste. House models were presented much in the same way as models of cars displayed on the lot, shiny new features added for each new season. Draftsmen were sent off to find acceptable and popular old housing types and reduce them to sizes that would qualify for government support. In 1949 architect Samuel Glaser took a seventeenth-century design – the Cape Cod cottage, already popular – and produced a more compact form with a price under $10,000.

Many first-time buyers were overwhelmed when they realized they could stop being rental tenants or living in their parents' houses and become homeowners instead. The increasingly efficient real estate machine provided homes not only for the first-timers but for those who were soon ready to enter the move-up market. The cheap Cape Cods made homeowners out of people who within years were ready to trade up to a larger, brighter, newer home. The exciting little suburban home of the 1940s became merely a starter home, a stepping stone to something bigger and better. With luck, the first house would have a resale value higher than the initial price and it would prove to be not an end in itself but a means to a greater end.

All levels of government as well as the banks encourage people to become homeowners. The construction of homes is viewed as a leading indicator of national prosperity, right up there with the production of motor vehicles. Numerous industries rely on the construction industry, including producers of cement, windows and doors, and lumber. Buying a home also triggers the purchase of many other consumer products such as furniture, draperies, dishes, hardware, and tools. A great deal depends on the homebuilding industry, such as the provision of jobs and services, and the manufacture and distribution of materials. The industry most assuredly produces homes in which people live. It also creates a product which plays a vital role both in national economies and in the personal finances of every household.

The arrival of the baby boomers on the homebuying scene was the most joyous time for builders since the end of the Second World War. The boomers first dipped their toes into the homeownership market in the early 1980s. Conforming to the general pattern according to which people move out of the parental home at around the age of twenty and live as rental tenants for the next ten to fifteen years before buying their first home, the boomers entered the housing market in the late 1960s, driving down apartment vacancy rates and sending up rents. They began to buy homes a bit later than expected, in the early 1980s, delayed by the recession and by prohibitively high interest rates. But when they began to buy in earnest, the housing market exploded and house prices rose steeply.

The average new house has expanded in size from about 1,500 square feet in the mid-1970s to over 2,000 square feet. Only one-fifth of new homes had two and a half bathrooms then; today half of all new homes have at least two full bathrooms and a powder room. The boomers seem to want more than their parents. Those who have college educations and good jobs and high incomes have seen more of the world and its attractions and have developed a taste for luxury. Although they have smaller families than those they grew up in, the boomers want more space in the home for their own families. Many start their homeowning careers in houses equivalent to the second or third homes that their parents had bought. They load their homes with amenities and features which proclaim, "We've made it – we have arrived."

Homes have taken on monstrous shapes and dimensions. Even though larger homes are a contradiction to the demographic portrait of a shrinking household, buyers seem to want as many bedrooms and guest rooms as possible. New rooms and new names for rooms have been devised to fill up all this desired space. When a room is created without any particular use, it is designated a *bonus room*. Another recent invention of developers is the *leisure room*. Bathrooms are no longer places merely for satisfying physical needs but have become sensual retreats, rooms for relaxation and pleasure, outfitted with whirlpool baths, multiple shower heads, heat lamps, vast expanses of mirror, and enough marble to satisfy a Roman emperor. Master bedrooms are not complete unless they have *two* walk-in closets now, one for him and one for her. Since builders have an unerring sense of what buyers want, these features are provided not only in expensive homes but in modified, miniaturized versions in more modestly priced homes.

Philip Langdon, author of the book *A Better Place to Live* and of numerous articles on contemporary housing design, analyses the current trends in homebuilding and the attitudes of homeowners to their investments. In the article "Dissecting the American House," Langdon writes: "It is features – double-height entrances, oversize bathtubs, sprawling master retreats – that builders use to win customers. And for this, American consumers pay dearly, surrendering not just their money but much of the satisfaction that a well-designed house can deliver." He describes many of the features used to woo and entice homebuyers by offering the illusion of material success: a multiplicity of complicated rooflines, a variety of different window shapes (including the pseudo-Palladian window surmounted by the essential semi-circle of glass), the soaring foyer, angled walls, stepped ceilings, three-car garages, a "great room" (combined kitchen/living room), "master retreats" (combined bedroom/bath/sitting area) – all of which "share the same bombastic yearning for super-deluxe effect." Langdon explains how a significant amount of production and custom house design is undertaken not by architects but by "building designers" who "view houses much as homeowners without architectural training tend to do: as a succession of features to be added together until the budget is exhausted."

In an earlier article, entitled simply "The American House," Langdon writes: "When some builders talk about craftsmanship and 'quality construction,' what they mean is expensive materials used here and there for emphasis, rather than consistently meticulous design and installation of whatever materials are used. The realtors' phrase 'curb appeal' means just what it suggests: many houses intent on charming the customer are not meant to be examined close up." He goes on to describe a situation where the housing consumer has developed an attitude much like that of a spoiled child's, a situation which provides superficial happiness at the expense of quality: "The balance within the American home has been shifting away from the pleasure of genuine materials well crafted and toward the satisfactions of mass-produced objects that fit into the family room, the kitchen, and the bath. Thus we can acquire comforts that were once unimaginable, yet complain that houses aren't built as well as they used to be." As a way out of this mess in the housing business caused by the culture of consumerism, Langdon recommends a rethink of the design of interior space combined with the elimination of useless features. He suggests that the size of houses be reduced in order to create "a smaller, but more usable and more satisfying dwelling." He adds: "American houses ought to incorporate both the technical and the social progress of the past 50 years and the admired qualities of well-crafted pre-World War II houses."

There was a time when most new homeowners used to be happy just to have a home. Today's purchasers of new homes are not content unless they can play an active role in as many phases of the home's design and construction as possible. Choice is offered in the selection of features and characteristics which used to be standard: kitchen cabinetry and fixtures, carpets and other floor coverings, lighting arrangements, sinks and taps and toilets. The personalization of a home – especially on a street where the homes can have a similar appearance, such as rowhouses – is certainly a desirable quality. The media encourage people to stand out, to express their individuality, to fulfil their needs. But when does the loading down of a home with amenities, whether they are security systems and central vacuums or indoor barbecues and spa baths, begin to work against homeowners when they want to sell? Too many extras and an excess of personalization could very well make a home undesirable to potential buyers. In the headlong rush to create a home that is comfortable and luxurious, individualized and creative, some owners may in fact be reducing the resale value of their homes, a consumer nightmare which would appall them if only they were to realize the ultimate effect of yet another skylight installation or the addition of a portico entrance with columns.

Where do people get some of the ideas for their homes? The print media is certainly one of the sources. This category includes not just the home and decor sections of the weekend paper but the glossy pages of hundreds of magazines devoted to design, style, architecture, home renovation, carpentry, even travel. The magazine *Architectural Digest* is read by close to a million people, mostly middle-to-upper class and in the twenty-five-to-forty-four age group. Many people read such publications to remain informed, to keep abreast of the latest developments in the architectural world, to provide themselves with high-quality images and text on stimulating design projects. But many readers also open these magazines for pure fun, to dream, to fantasize. Architecture and design publications are hardly recent inventions. A typical article in *House Beautiful* from the time of its founding over a hundred years ago would describe the lavish home of a business magnate, comment on the historical context of its style, and use words far more than pictures to get the job done. Far different in substance and technique from our present-day shelter magazines, it would still serve many of the same purposes: current information, entertainment value, fodder for dreaming and fantasy.

More directly accessible perhaps, and closer to the pure realm of fantasy, are the movie mags and the home and style weeklies and monthlies which give us glimpses into the homes of the rich and famous. Such magazines deliver photos of movie stars and celebrities in their home environments, casually relaxing, lolling by the pool, adjusting a cushion or curtain edge, looking down over the valley from the terrace. Readers hungrily devour every detail: number of square feet, dollars spent, colour schemes chosen, stated influences, type of art, names of trees, size of hot tub and pool. It is impossible to know exactly why people are so fascinated by the homes of the people they follow in the news and movies. Maybe their homes reveal additional information about their lives, something to add to their allure and to our obsession with them. Perhaps the reader wants confirmation that the super-rich really *are* different, that they inhabit some alien realm of extreme wealth and privilege, exemplified neatly by their homes which are so very unlike the homes of the common people. Or maybe people are actually hunting for ways in which they can model their own homes on what they see in the magazines. Readers may believe that they are merely flapping pages and dreaming while in fact they are stashing away a host of little design and decorating tips to be put to use on the next visit to the furniture store or renovation emporium.

Television is another huge source of ideas for what a home can or could be like. People don't watch TV for hours on end without absorbing some sense of the home furnishings and styles they observe on show after show about "typical" North American life, not to mention the commercials which actively encourage the viewer to shop at this mattress store or that furniture warehouse. There is a certain interior layout common to most television sitcoms, now decades old: a central living room, stairs visible in the rear, front door to the right, kitchen door to the left, and a big sofa in the middle facing an unseen TV which is where we, the audience, sit: on *our* side of the TV screen. Generations of television watchers have seen the style of furnishings and decor change within this unchanging landscape, marking the years with the passing technologies and fashions. The devotion of certain groups to their beloved shows can be found in websites dedicated to favourite shows that have long gone off the air. Baby boomers who used to love *Bewitched*, for instance, can access the website for the house at 1164 Morning Glory Circle and check out the floor plans and peruse every decoration detail down to the colour of the moldings in the hall or the style of chairs in the dining room.

Who can say to what extent TV shows set the tone for the interior design of many homes? Do boomers access such websites out of nostalgia, out of an attempt to revisit their own childhood homes from the 1960s, or are they actually trawling for retro tips, for ironic touches to their own post-sixties, post-suburban, post-*Bewitched* homes? Does the decor in current TV shows merely reflect things as they are beyond the screen, or does it serve to dictate to legions of watchers the way they themselves can fix up their places? No one could say definitively that a particular show has invented a certain style or decor, but there is no denying the effect television has in promoting a certain look as hip or cool or, at the very least, desirable. Once we are entangled in the commercial realm of television, we are involved in a complex milieu of screaming advertisements and subconscious suggestion. Take away from it what we will, we are all affected to some degree by what other people (producers, writers, manufacturers, sellers) want us to see.

Of all the choices homeowners make, perhaps the most significant – in terms of its effect on the value of the home and on the staying power of that value – is the selection of neighbourhood. Forced to decide which is more important, the quality of the neighbourhood or the house itself, two-thirds of homeowners consider the neighbourhood to be the primary concern. Most people first pick an area to live in and then look for a home there. The choice of neighbourhood depends on a vast range of factors: personal history, household taste and preference, job and income, quality of education, security. When people choose a home, they need "only" take into account price, layout, age of the house: characteristics which link the homeowners' needs and financial abilities with a particular structure on a particular plot of land. These are weighty considerations indeed, and they can provide a potential homeowner with huge amounts of stress and grief, but at least they involve real estate which comes to be owned and inhabited by a single household. The neighbourhood, on the other hand, is an entity which exists beyond the control and ownership of any one buyer. People considering the purchase of a home therefore do well to look long and hard at the surroundings: the quality of the other structures, the types of households which inhabit them, the overall tone of the neighbourhood. The value of a home is higher in a place where many people wish to live, where general agreement declares that, yes, this is a good neighbourhood. Of course, the homes may be grand and their prices high, but that would be expected in the part of town where residents have the strongest motives for maintaining the status quo.

No one can blame homeowners for wanting to maintain and ultimately to increase the value of their homes. Municipal zoning mechanisms exist to protect these real estate values and to prevent the occurrence of anything that might diminish the investments of homeowners. Zoning bylaws ensure that the house next door to your own cannot be torn down so that an all-night food take-out stand can be built instead. Zoning prescribes the density of a neighbourhood as well as land coverage, which determines how many homes can be built within a certain area and how big those homes must be. In the end, zoning operates to shield homeowners from perceived challenges to their property and, on another level, to establish neighbourhoods which are segregated by household income and housing type. Put crudely, people in expensive homes do not want an inexpensive home belonging to a person with a low income next door. Such a hideous circumstance, they reason, would lower the value of their own property. They would prefer people more like themselves who live in comparable houses.

People are naturally afraid of the unexpected and the uncertain, and zoning bylaws are based on the fears and expectations of homeowners. Most communities, for instance, do not permit the mixing of housing types – single-family houses and multi-unit complexes on the same street, for instance – because of the received notion that the lower-priced homes will bring down the value of the higher-priced homes. Even though mixed housing types could lead to a vibrant neighbourhood suited to the changed make-up and new demands of our society, this mixing is seen as a bad thing. It is as though homebuyers cannot be trusted to distinguish between a rowhouse and a two-storey detached house and the types of households which would be apt candidates for living in them. These different types of homes, the tradition goes, must be kept separate so as not to confuse and infuriate the citizenry.

The not-in-my-backyard (NIMBY) attitude towards the prospect of undesirable elements moving into the neighbourhood is not a new phenomenon and is directly related to the homeowner's urge to banish any threats to life and property. No one wants a nuclear waste facility at the end of the block or a new meat-rendering plant in the area. The problem with the urge to keep out certain people and housing types is when the bottom line becomes the creation and preservation of a neighbourhood composed solely of similar residences and inhabitants. The more homogeneous the suburb, the more likely it is that "alternative" (i.e., non-traditional) households and any form of housing that does not conform to the picket-fence model (i.e., apartment blocks or semi-detached homes or rowhouses) will be viewed as foreign and dangerous. NIMBYism understandably gains support among the members of a community when the cause is opposition to the construction of a prison or the opening of a new garbage dump, but it shows its pernicious side when neighbours band together to prevent the implementation of useful projects which challenge their own perceived notions of the status quo.

Residents in a Long Island community of prewar homes organized themselves against the plan to build a two-storey, ninety-unit apartment building for the elderly on the site of a three-acre school athletic field. The developers of the project wanted to obtain a rezoning of the site from single-family residential to the "golden age" classification to permit housing for the elderly at a density of up to thirty units per acre, but the NIMBY group felt that the project would bring unwanted traffic, noise and commercial activity to the area, and open the door to further zoning changes which would fundamentally change the nature of their neighbourhood: single-family homes with a suburban way of life. In Georgia a group of homeowners fought (unsuccessfully) to prevent the introduction of a manufactured home into their neighbourhood. The mobile home was over 1,500 square feet in size, built by a state-licensed manufacturer, was to be put on a permanent foundation and would sit on a lot just under two acres: all of which conformed to the zoning requirements for the area. Even so, the residents felt that the proposed form of housing was not up to their idea of proper standards.

A single woman in Connecticut who received federal and state funds to assist her family searched for an appropriate home for her ten foster children, some of whom were disabled. Many of the people in the affluent neighbourhood filed a lawsuit and acted to obtain a temporary restraining order to keep her and her family out of their area, alleging that the presence of the children (who were non-white) would diminish the attractiveness and value of their property. The neighbours maintained that they had no problem with the fact that the mother was a single woman or with the ethnicity of the children; they were simply concerned with the use of the home and the potential for unlimited numbers of children. Property owners in an Ontario community near Hamilton won a public hearing to protest against a fifty-two-unit, four-building development funded by the provincial ministry of housing when they found out that the housing would be subsidized and was for Native Canadian residents. They complained about the effect on the value of their homes and of increased traffic. Some even suggested placing "For Sale" signs on their own homes as a form of protest.

Many homeowners oppose the introduction of affordable housing into their neighbourhoods. Under the mistaken impression that "affordable housing" is just a diversionary term for "poor people's housing," they agitate against its construction because they fear an invasion of welfare recipients into their community, little realizing that many people who get caught in the mortgage squeeze or who would rather not devote all their spare cash to housing expenses (for example, teachers, nurses, young professionals) are all candidates for affordable housing.

The ultimate neighbourhood exercise in exclusion and segregation is the gated community, the contemporary equivalent of a walled city or fortress. There are approximately twenty thousand gated communities in the United States, with a total of three million housing units. Some are luxury communities, others retirement enclaves, and the rest are middle-class subdivisions. Edward J. Blakely and Mary Gail Snyder, authors of the book *Fortress America*, write in the article "Forting Up: Gated Communities in the United States" on the relationship of these neighbourhoods to the later evolution of the suburbs:

> These developments are descendants not just of a tradition of elite enclaves, but of decades of suburban design and public land use policy. Gates are firmly within the suburban tradition of street patterns and zoning designed to reduce the access of nonresidents and increase homogeneity. Gates enhance and harden the suburban-ness of the suburbs, and they attempt to suburbanize the city … As the suburbs age and become more dense and more diverse, they are encountering problems once thought of as urban – crime, vandalism, disinvestment, and blight. Gated communities seek to counter these trends by maintaining the ambiance of exclusivity and safety the suburbs once promised. They exist not just to wall out crime or traffic or strangers, but to lock in economic position. It is hoped that greater control over the neighbourhood will mean greater stability in property values for homeowners.

Gated communities exclude all those deemed inadequate to the standards of the enclosed members: the poor, the unemployed, the working class – in other words, the great unwashed public. The undesirables are kept out through two basic methods: the gates themselves, and the rules and restrictions of the homeowners' association which ensure that the inhabitants follow a tight code of behaviour and activity which in turn ensure that only a particular kind of household would want to live there to begin with.

Many gated communities are marketed as small towns within the context of a larger city, as a special place which has a neighbourly spirit and strong community values. Some of these developments in and around Toronto, Ontario, are marketed as "Florida-style" gated communities, to emphasize the aura of luxury and exclusivity, the promise of comfort in a retirement setting. The fact is that such places are cut off from a connection with the larger community. The inhabitants come to resent all those who live outside and they feel indifferent to the concerns and problems of the larger city and world. Housing values and a supposed sense of security are paramount.

With regard to the segregationist aspect of gated communities – the elevation of self-interest over a true spirit of community – Blakely and Snyder write:

> Residents buy more than a house which suits their needs and preferences when they buy into a gated development. They also buy into a set of private amenities and services that are exclusively theirs. Community is a commodity in these developments. Residents are buying a lifestyle, an environment, a set of services, and a structure for interaction with their neighbours … The exclusionary ideal of gated communities arises from the status associated

with social distance. This pattern of social distance has long been a goal of American settlement patterns – the suburbs were built on separation and segregation. The suburban pattern reinforces the splintering of community with social separation and physical walls.

*Community is a commodity.*
*Residents are buying a lifestyle.*
*The suburbs were built on separation and segregation.*

When we take an honest look at the way our lives and housing have evolved in the last half-century or so, we find that the priorities underlying the creation and acquisition of homes have tended towards isolation and profit-making and away from any ideals such as neighbourliness and integration. Community used to be something that people developed and nurtured, not purchased. A lifestyle was cultivated or adopted, not bought. Neighbourhoods were for bringing people together, not for forcing them apart. Homeowners have always considered their homes as properties to be valued, and most people have never been averse to making money when the opportunity presented itself, but as members of a community and society, they have always been duty bound to respect the rights and privileges of others.

In our present age of prosperity and growth, in the adventurous decades following the Second World War, we have witnessed the deliberate polarization of housing types and housing users – fine, large homes for some, inadequate housing for others. The fine, large homes keep getting finer and larger, while the inadequate housing keeps getting smaller and meaner. We put a price tag not only on the home but on the community. We sell the neighbourhood and all the facilities. If people lack the wherewithal to ante up, they are not even allowed to sit at the table. In short, something distinctly unfriendly and unneighbourly has been going on. We are sacrificing community for a commodity.

## Afterword:

# Where Do We Go from Here?

Recent decades have been a time of cascading changes that have left their mark on homes and the urban fabric. Sometimes it is impossible to know which issues and trends are important and which will turn out to be insignificant. At the turn of the twenty-first century, certain issues are more noticeable than others. They command more play in the media, they attract corporate and government notice, they affect public and personal agendas. Listing the big topics is risky, but we can venture to say that the make-up of our society, economic wellbeing, and lifestyle choices are subjects worth examining when we wonder which forces will shape our homes in the years to come.

We begin this final reflection where the book itself began: with the society we live in. As the definition of the family continues to evolve, and as the variety of households who buy homes expands, the design and use of our homes also change. The cause of sensible housing will take a strong step forward when builders, developers, advertisers, and the public at large accept, once and for all, that there is no such thing as a typical North American household. Many providers of homes already realize that a more equitable – and profitable – approach to housing is to assume a multiplicity of household types. Suburban houses aimed squarely at a family of two parents and more than two children certainly find takers, but they also omit as many households as they include. The traditional family still does exist but it is matched by a fascinating array of other types of homeowners: single parents, same-sex couples, empty-nesters, singles, childless married couples. To design and build housing for only half the market makes bad business sense and bad social sense.

We can only speculate on the ultimate fate of the oversized suburban home. As long as it continues to be a potent image of successful achievement in life, it will remain part of the North American Dream. This does not mean that we have to endorse it. Being attuned to the current reality means a shift in expectations even when one attempts to follow the same patterns as one's parents. A prime example of the person who experiences this kind of change is the boomer who was brought up in a large family house with many brothers and sisters. That same boomer, as a middle-aged adult today, may be divorced and only sees the kids on the weekend, or may be married but has only two children. This person may earn a good living but has very little security in a contract job, or may have a steady job that simply does not pay too well. The spouse may also work, a marked difference from the 1950s and 1960s scenario where dad marched off to work alone and paid the mortgage alone. Whatever the circumstances of this person's life, it is increasingly likely these days that the boomer in question does not live in the same type of housing as in childhood. He or she may just as easily live in a rowhouse or in a condo on the twenty-third floor or in an apartment or duplex. Many people who find themselves accommodated outside of a single-family detached house in the suburbs have not come down in the world. Far from it: they have merely carved out a new way for themselves in a changed world.

As households shrink in size and as the number of homes occupied by single people increases, the need for compact homes is one solution. No one wants to force people into smaller homes. Buy as much space as you need and want. But building smaller means that more people can afford to become homeowners. If households are getting smaller all the time, why have single-family homes grown by one-third in size over the last twenty years? Why can we not think *compact* without feeling that we have failed? There is no shame in ending the drift towards expansion and waste.

Homes with greater flexibility are also an answer to many of our shifting requirements. The issue of flexibility involves the notion that a home can be designed with the built-in capacity for change, and it addresses a vital need which many homeowners feel: that they would rather their homes adapt to new conditions in their lives than be forced to adapt themselves to a new home because of a changed situation in life. Many people are saddened and even disgusted by the throw-away, disposable culture in which they live. Homeowners do not just toss away their homes like a candy wrapper or chip bag when they move – they sell them, perhaps for a profit. But a great number resent having to abandon their complete home environment (the house, the backyard, the neighbourhood, the community) because their household is different from when they originally bought the home. If the option exists to rearrange rooms without huge expense and mess, or to purchase and take over the floor above or below without major structural work, or to reduce the total square footage by selling off a portion after the kids leave home, then many people would be spared the strain and burden of moving. On a scale of life events, moving house ranks near the top in terms of stress and trauma, right up there with divorce and death of a loved one. If people can be spared that trial and annoyance, and if they can be left in peace in the home of their own choosing for as long as they want, then those responsible for the design and construction of their homes can be said to have done a good job.

A vital component of change is loosening up some of our definitions and expectations. Rather than let a neighbourhood of large older houses go downhill because the market for them has changed, it would benefit both the community and prospective individual homeowners if zoning bylaws were amended to allow for new uses and boundaries. Split the large home into two: make a duplex out of a house originally built as a single-family home. Allowing a split extends the opportunity for ownership to a greater number of buyers; the whole house could be purchased by a single household or the house could be divided into halves, each half available to buyers who would otherwise not be interested.

Cycles of economic boom and bust are nothing new, but recognizing that simple fact does not make life much easier for any of us. As personal finances fluctuate in accordance with shifting fortunes, the majority of potential home buyers find it more and more difficult to purchase a home. We maintain that homeownership ought to be available to everybody. Governments at all levels have taken less responsibility for housing in the past several years, so the private sector will have to pick up the slack. Innovation will be a key ingredient to the potential success of builders. Smaller homes, efficient design and use of materials, the offer of choice to buyers so that they can select and pay for what they want and need – these are major considerations for today's housing industry.

Environmental awareness is another lesson of the past few decades that has been incorporated into the production of our homes. Suburbia was the result of the need to house many people quickly and cheaply. Abundant land, affordable cars, and cheap gas allowed us to extend the boundaries of our cities into areas where only farms and forests once existed. But we came to recognize that natural resources are not limitless, that cars pollute, and sprawl can be an ugly thing. There really is no alternative to building denser and using our resources more carefully.

Our spending habits, as well as the way we seem to enjoy accessorizing our lives with gadgets and toys, has led to a lifestyle of heavy consumption. New domestic technologies are introduced to improve and facilitate our lives, but there comes a point when we must ask: *Do we really need all this stuff?* Have we succumbed to the coercion of advertising, or the temptations of bright and glittery trinkets, or the allure of shopping as a form of therapy or consolation? We would find more space in our homes if we bought less junk to stuff inside. Lifestyle trends and habits are hard to categorize and even more difficult to assign any sort of value or judgment on their quality. What the life inside a home will be like is determined by each individual household. We can only hope that people live responsibly and happily, without unnecessary hardship and waste.

Options, choice, and flexibility are features in a home that extend beyond the nuts and bolts of foundations and ceilings. The greater the diversity in our society, the wider must be our range of selection. And within each individual life resides the potential for any number of lifestyles and directions. We should not be limited by a narrow assortment of housing types. We do ourselves wrong by providing homes that suit only a portion of our society. Our homes must suit our lives: all of our lives, for their entire duration.

# Bibliography

## Note on Sources

The original bibliography was almost seventy pages long and contained references to every book, journal, magazine, newspaper article, database, and website consulted in the course of researching this book. To print such a long and varied list would be both tedious and confusing. Moreover, website addresses change or disappear with alarming frequency, rendering impossible any attempt to provide a current list. We have therefore opted to provide a selection of our sources, arranged by chapter, as a way of offering a more manageable and comprehensible portrait of the research work we undertook. All websites listed are included only in the introduction section, although we referred to them repeatedly throughout the succeeding chapters; they refer to general addresses consulted from the years 1997 to 2002.

## Introduction: The Accelerated Present

*American Demographics*: www.demographics.com

Canada Mortgage and Housing Corporation: www.cmhc-schl.gc.ca

National Association of Home Builders: www.nahb.com

National Center for Health Statistics: www.cdc.gov/nchs

Population Reference Bureau, Inc.: www.prb.org

Statistics Canada: www.statcan.ca

United States Census Bureau: www.census.gov

United States Department of Housing and Urban Development:
www.hud.gov

United States Department of Labor (Occupational Safety and Health
Administration): www.osha-slc.gov

United States Department of Transportation (Bureau of Transportation
Statistics): www.bts.gov

United States Environmental Protection Agency: www.epa.gov


### Chapter 1: What We Eat, Where We Eat

*Abitare.* "Furniture for the New Kitchen" (June 1990): 177.

Beyer, Glenn H. *Housing and Society.* New York: Macmillan, 1965.

Brent, Ruth, and Benyamin Schwarz, eds. *Popular American Housing:
A Reference Guide.* Westport, CT: Greenwood Press, 1995.

Conran, Terence. *The Kitchen Book.* New York: Crown Publishers Inc., 1977.

Cowan, Ruth Schwartz. *More Work for Mother: The Ironies of Household
Technology from the Open Hearth to the Microwave.* New York: Basic Books,
1983.

Desmond, Kevin. *A Timetable of Inventions and Discoveries.* New York:
M. Evans & Company, Inc., 1986.

Doran, Susan. "Kitchens of Tomorrow," *Homes and Cottages* 8, 5 (August
1998): 70–5.

Hayden, Dolores. *Redesigning the American Dream: The Future of Housing,
Work, and Family Life.* New York: W.W. Norton & Company, 1984.

Heeney, William H. *Fresher than Fresh: The Pioneering Days of Food Preservation by the Miracle of Quick Freezing.* Ottawa: Ministry of Agriculture, 1984.

Leaversuch, Robert D. "Hunger for 'Ready' Food Stimulates New Options in Barrier Packaging," *Modern Plastics* (November 1997): 70–3.

Ravetz, Alison, with Richard Turkington. *The Place of Home: English Domestic Environments, 1914–2000.* London: E & FN Spon, 1995.

Selke, Susan. *Packaging and the Environment: Alternatives, Trends and Solutions.* Lancaster, PA: Technomic Publishing Co., Inc., 1990.

Strasser, Susan. *Never Done: A History of American Housework.* New York: Pantheon Books, 1982.

Walley, Joan E. *The Kitchen.* London: Constable & Company, 1960.

Wentling, James. *Designing a Place Called Home: Reordering the Suburbs.* New York: Chapman & Hall, 1995.

## Chapter 2: Webs and Wires

Alexander, Alison. "The Effect of Media on Family Interaction," in Dolf Zillmann, Jennings Bryant, and Aletha C. Huston, eds., *Media, Children and the Family.* Hillsdale, NJ: Lawrence Erlbaum Associates, 1994, 51–60.

Alexander, Karen. "Building a SOHO: It's Not as Easy as you Think," *Office Systems* 14, 2 (December 1997): 30–2.

Anderson, D.R., and P.A. Collins. *The Impact on Children's Education: Television's Influence on Cognitive Development.* Washington, DC: U.S. Department of Education, 1988.

Anderson, D.R., S.R. Levin, and E.P. Lorch. "The Effects of TV Program Pacing on the Behavior of Preschool Children," *AV Communication Review* 25 (1977): 154–66.

Armour, Stephanie. "Blame it on Downsizing, E-mail, Laptops and Dual-career Families," *USA Today* (13 March 1998): B1.

Boris, Eileen, and Cynthia R. Daniels, eds. *Homework: Historical and Contemporary Perspectives on Paid Labor at Home*. Chicago: University of Illinois Press, 1989.

Boris, Eileen, and Elisabeth Prügl, eds. *Homeworkers in Global Perspective: Invisible No More*. New York: Routledge, 1996.

Coe, Lewis. *The Telephone and Its Several Inventors*. Jefferson, NC: McFarland & Company, Inc., 1995.

Fisher, David E., and Marshall Jon Fisher. *Tube: The Invention of Television*. Washington, DC: Counterpoint, 1996.

Friedman, Avi, David Krawitz, Jasmin S. Fréchette, Cyrus M. Bilimoria, and Doug Raphael. *The Next Home*. Montreal: McGill University School of Architecture Affordable Homes Program, 1996.

Gates, Bill, with Nathan Myhrvold and Peter Rinearson. *The Road Ahead*. New York: Viking, 1995.

Hillman, Judy. *Telelifestyles and the Flexicity: The Impact of the Electronic Home*. Shankill, Ireland: European Foundation for the Improvement of Living and Working Conditions, 1993.

Huston, Aletha C., Dolf Zillmann, and Jennings Bryant. "Media Influence, Public Policy, and the Family," in Dolf Zillmann, Jennings Bryant and Aletha C. Huston, eds., *Media, Children and the Family*. Hillsdale, NJ: Lawrence Erlbaum Associates, 1994, 3–18.

Huston, Aletha C. et al. *Big World, Small Screen: The Role of Television in American Society*. Lincoln, NE: University of Nebraska Press, 1992.

Jones, Gerard. *Honey, I'm Home! Sitcoms: Selling the American Dream*. New York: Grove Press, Inc., 1992.

Kubey, Robert. "Media Implications for the Quality of Family Life," in Dolf Zillmann, Jennings Bryant and Aletha C. Huston, eds., *Media, Children and the Family*. Hillsdale, NJ: Lawrence Erlbaum Associates, 1994, 61–70.

Lodish, Leonard et al. "How TV Advertising Works," *Journal of Marketing Research* (May 1995): 125–40.

Mack, Dana. *The Assault on Parenthood: How Our Culture Undermines the Family.* New York: Simon & Schuster, 1997.

McCune, Jenny C. "Telecommuting Revisited," *Management Review* 87, 2 (February 1998): 10–16.

Moran, Rosalyn. *The Electronic Home: Social and Spatial Aspects.* Shankill, Ireland: European Foundation for the Improvement of Living and Working Conditions, 1993.

Paul, Donna. *The Home Office Book.* New York: Artisan, 1996.

Postman, Neil. *The Disappearance of Childhood.* New York: Vintage Books, 1994.

Risher, Howard. "Behind the Big Picture: Employment Trends in the 1990s," *Compensation & Benefits Review* (January/February 1997): 8–12.

Spigel, Lynn. *Make Room for TV: Television and the Family Ideal in Postwar America.* Chicago: University of Chicago Press, 1992.

Ward, Peter. *A History of Domestic Space: Privacy and the Canadian Home.* Vancouver: UBC Press, 1999.

Williams, Trevor I. *The Triumph of Invention: A History of Man's Technological Genius.* London: Macdonald & Co. (Publishers) Ltd., 1987.

Wolman, William, and Anne Colamosa. *The Judas Economy: The Triumph of Capital and the Betrayal of Work.* New York: Addison-Wesley Publishing Company, 1997.

## Chapter 3: Buy New or Renovate?

Ahluwalia, Gopal, and Angela Shackford. "Life Expectancy of Building Materials," *Jonathan Press* 2, 1 (October-March 1997–8).

Canada Mortgage and Housing Corporation. *Building Materials for the*

*Environmentally Hypersensitive*. Ottawa: Canada Mortgage and Housing Corporation, 1995.

– *The Changing Housing Industry in Canada, 1946–2001*. Ottawa: Canada Mortgage and Housing Corporation, 1988.

Canadian Home Builders' Association. *Residential Renovation: Industry Framework*. Ottawa: Canadian Home Builders' Association, 1996.

Cromley, Elizabeth Collins. "A History of American Beds and Bedrooms, 1890–1930," in Jessica H. Foy and Thomas J. Schlereth, eds., *American Home Life, 1890–1930*. Knoxville, TN: University of Tennessee Press, 1992, 122–44.

Dean, John P., and Simon Breines. *The Book of Houses*. New York: Crown Publishers, 1946.

Elliott, Cecil D. *Technics and Architecture: The Development of Materials and Systems for Buildings*. Cambridge, MA: The MIT Press, 1992.

Ennals, Peter, and Deryck W. Holdsworth. *Homeplace: The Making of the Canadian Dwelling over Three Centuries*. Toronto: University of Toronto Press, 1998.

Ford, Katherine Morrow, and Thomas H. Creighton. *Quality Budget Houses*. New York: Reinhold Publishing Corporation, 1954.

Friedel, Robert. "Scarcity and Promise: Materials and American Domestic Culture During World War II," in Donald Albrecht, ed., *World War II and the American Dream: How Wartime Building Changed a Nation*. Washington, DC: National Building Museum, 1995, 42–89.

Geary, Don. *Roofs and Siding: A Practical Guide*. Reston, Virginia: Reston Publishing Company, Inc., 1978.

Hoyle, Robert J., Jr., and Frank E. Woeste. *Wood Technology in the Design of Structures* (5th ed.). Ames, IA: Iowa State University Press, 1989.

Lanspery, Susan and Joan Hyde, eds. *Staying Put: Adapting the Places Instead of the People*. Amityville, NY: Baywood Publishing Company, Inc., 1997.

Lea, Michael J. "Innovation and the Cost of Mortgage Credit," *Housing Policy Debate* 7, 1 (1996), 147–74.

McKellar, James. "Building Technology and the Production Process," in John R. Miron, ed., *House, Home and Community: Progress in Housing Canadians, 1945–1986.* Ottawa: Canada Mortgage and Housing Corporation, 1993.

Nelson, George, and Henry Wright. *Tomorrow's House.* New York: Simon and Schuster, 1945.

Pantelopoulos, Maria D. "Small Living Spaces: A Study of Space Management in Wartime Homes in Montreal." M. Arch. thesis. Montreal: McGill University, 1993.

Reed, Peter S. "Enlisting Modernism," in Donald Albrecht, ed., *World War II and the American Dream: How Wartime Building Changed a Nation.* Washington, DC: National Building Museum, 1995, 2–41.

Ritchie, T. et al. *Canada Builds: 1867–1967.* Toronto: University of Toronto Press, 1967.

R.S. Means Company Inc. *Residential Square Foot Costs, 1997 Edition.* Kingston, MA: Construction Publishers & Consultants, 1996.

Slaten, Vince. *Did Monkeys Invent the Monkey Wrench?* New York: Simon & Schuster, 1996.

Walsh, H. Vandervoot. "House Building Materials Reappraised," *Architectural Record* (November 1947): 115–120.

Wright, Gwendolyn. *Building the Dream: A Social History of Housing in America.* New York: Pantheon Books, 1981.

**Chapter 4: Living with Kids**

Alexander, A., M.S. Ryan, and P. Munoz. "Creating a Learning Context: Investigations on the Interaction of Siblings During Co-viewing," *Critical Studies in Mass Communication* 1 (1984): 345–64.

Bartlett, Sheridan N. "Housing as a Factor in the Socialization of Children: A Critical Review of the Literature," *Merrill-Palmer Quarterly* 43, 2 (April 1997): 169–98.

Booth, Alan. "Quality of Children's Family Interaction in relation to Residential Type and Household Crowding," in Joachim F. Wohlwill and Willem van Vliet, eds., *Habitats for Children: The Impacts of Density*. Hillsdale, NJ: Lawrence Erlbaum Associates, 1985, 145–64.

Calvert, Karin. *Children in the House: The Material Culture of Early Childhood, 1600–1900*. Boston: Northeastern University Press, 1992.

Chawla, Louise. "Homes for Children in a Changing Society," in Ervin H. Zube and Gary T. Moore, eds. *Advances in Environment, Behavior and Design*. New York: Plenum Press, 1991, 187–230.

Cooper Marcus, Clare and Wendy Sarkissian. *Housing as if People Mattered: Site Design Guidelines for Medium-Density Family Housing*. Berkeley: University of California Press, 1986.

Cross, Gary. *Kids' Stuff: Toys and the Changing World of American Childhood*. Cambridge, MA: Harvard University Press, 1997.

Franck, Karen A., and Sherry Ahrentzen, eds., *New Households, New Housing*. New York: Van Nostrand Reinhold, 1989.

Johnson, Laura C. "The Developmental Implications of Home Environments," in Carol Simon Weinstein and Thomas G. David, eds., *Spaces for Children: The Built Environment and Child Development*. New York: Plenum Press, 1987, 139–57.

Maxwell, Lorraine E. "Multiple Effects of Home and Day Care Crowding," *Environment and Behavior* (July 1996): 494–511.

Opie, Iona, and Peter Opie. *Children's Games in Street and Playground*. London: Oxford University Press, 1969.

Schofield, Angela. *Toys in History*. East Sussex, England: Wayland Publishers, 1978.

Schoggen, Phil, and Maxine Schoggen. "Play, Exploration, and Density," in
Joachim F. Wohlwill and Willem van Vliet, eds., *Habitats for Children: The
Impacts of Density*. Hillsdale, NJ: Lawrence Erlbaum Associates, 1985,
77–96.

Sommerville, John. *The Rise and Fall of Childhood*. Beverly Hills: Sage Publications, 1982.

Stearns, Peter N. et al. "Children's Sleep: Sketching Historical Change,"
*Journal of Social History* (Winter 1996): 345–66.

van Vliet, Willem, and Joachim F. Wohlwill. "Habitats for Children: The
State of the Evidence," in *Habitats for Children: The Impacts of Density*.
Hillsdale, NJ: Lawrence Erlbaum Associates, 1985, 201–229.

Zeisel, John, and Polly Welch. *Housing Designed for Families: A Summary of
Research*. Cambridge, MA: Joint Center for Urban Studies, 1981.

Zinn, Hermann. "The Influence of Home Environments on the Socialization
of Children," *Ekistics: The Problems and Science of Human Settlements* 47,
281 (March/April 1980): 98–102.

**Chapter 5: Growing Old at Home**

Adler, Rick. "Stereotypes Won't Work with Seniors Anymore," *Advertising
Age* (11 November 1996): 32.

Baucom, Alfred H., with Robert J. Grosch. *Hospitality Design for the Graying
Generation: Meeting the Needs of a Growing Market*. New York: John Wiley
& Sons, Inc., 1996.

Canada Mortgage and Housing Corporation. *Environmental Competence
amongst Independent Elderly Households*. Ottawa: Canada Mortgage and
Housing Corporation, n.d.

– *Housing Choices for Older Canadians*. Ottawa: Canada Mortgage and Housing Corporation, n.d.

Gibler, Karen Martin, James R. Lumpkin, and George P. Moschis. "Mature

Consumer Awareness and Attitudes Toward Retirement Housing and Long-Term Care Alternatives," *The Journal of Consumer Affairs* 31, 1 (Summer 1997): 113–38.

Hansson, Robert O., and Bruce N. Carpenter. *Relationships in Old Age: Coping with the Challenge of Transition*. New York: The Guilford Press, 1994.

Heumann, Leonard F., and Duncan P. Boldy. "The Basic Benefits and Limitations of an Aging-in-Place Policy," in Leonard F. Heumann and Duncan P. Boldy, eds., *Aging in Place with Dignity: International Solutions Relating to the Low-Income and Frail Elderly*. Westport, CT: Praeger, 1993, 1–8.

Hunt, Michael E. "The Design of Supportive Environments for Older People," in Lenard W. Kaye and Abraham Monk, eds., *Congregate Housing for the Elderly: Theoretical, Policy, and Programmatic Perspectives*. New York: The Haworth Press, 1991, 127–40.

– et al. *Retirement Communities: An American Original*. New York: The Haworth Press, 1984.

National Advisory Council on Aging. *Housing an Aging Population: Guidelines for Development and Design*. Ottawa: Minister of Supply and Services Canada, 1987.

Pastalan, Leon A. "Sensory Changes and Environmental Behavior," *Design for Aging: A Comprehensive Package*. Washington, DC: American Institute of Architects/Association of Collegiate Schools of Architecture, 1992.

Pynoos, Jon, and Stephen Golant. "Housing and Living Arrangements for the Elderly," in Robert H. Binstock and Linda K. George, eds., *Handbook of Aging and the Social Sciences*, 4th ed. San Diego: Academic Press, 1995, 303–24.

Regnier, Victor, and Jon Pynoos, eds., *Housing the Aged: Design Directives and Policy Considerations*. New York: Elsevier Science Publishing Co., Inc., 1987.

Schiff, Myra. "Special Design Considerations: Developing and Marketing Retirement Housing." Toronto: Myra Schiff Consultants Limited, n.d.

Steinfeld, Edward. "Adapting Housing for Older Disabled People," *Design for Aging: A Comprehensive Package*. Washington, DC: American Institute of Architects/Association of Collegiate Schools of Architecture, 1992.

Sykes, James T. "Living Independently with Neighbors Who Care: Strategies to Facilitate Aging in Place," *Design for Aging: A Comprehensive Package*. Washington, DC: American Institute of Architects/Association of Collegiate Schools of Architecture, 1992.

Whiting, David, and Bill Woodwark. *A Senior's Home: Designs for Independent Living*. Edmonton, AB: Alberta Municipal Affairs, 1985.


### Chapter 6: Where Exactly Do We Live?

American Automobile Manufacturers Association. *Motor Vehicles Facts and Figures, 1995*. Washington, DC: American Automobile Manufacturers Association, 1995.

Canada Mortgage and Housing Corporation. *The Clean Air Guide*. Ottawa: Canada Mortgage and Housing Corporation, 1993.

Cohen, Lizabeth. "From Town Center to Shopping Center: The Reconfiguration of Community Marketplaces in Postwar America," *American Historical Review* (October 1996): 1050–81.

Donaldson, Gary A. *Abundance and Anxiety: America, 1945-1960*. Westport, CT: Praeger Publishers, 1997.

Duany, Andres, Elizabeth Plater-Zyberk, and Jeff Speck. *Suburban Nation: The Rise of Sprawl and the Decline of the American Dream*. New York: North Point Press, 2000.

Duany, Andres, and Elizabeth Plater-Zyberk. *Towns and Town-Making Principles*. New York: Rizzoli, 1991.

FitzGerald, Frances. *Cities on a Hill: A Journey through Contemporary American Cultures*. New York: Touchstone, 1986.

Garbarino, James. "Habitats for Children: An Ecological Perspective," in

Joachim F. Wohlwill and Willem van Vliet, eds., *Habitats for Children: The Impacts of Density*. Hillsdale, NJ: Lawrence Erlbaum Associates, 1985, 125–43.

Garvin, Alexander. *The American City: What Works, What Doesn't*. New York: McGraw-Hill Companies, 1996.

Hanchett, Thomas W. "U.S. Tax Policy and the Shopping-Center Boom of the 1950's and 1960's," *American Historical Review* (October 1996): 1082–1110.

Jackson, Kenneth T. "All the World's a Mall: Reflections on the Social and Economic Consequences of the American Shopping Center," *American Historical Review* (October 1996): 1111–21.

Kelbaugh, Doug. "The New Urbanism," *Journal of Architectural Education* 51, 2 (November 1997): 142–44.

Lucic, Katija. "Human Scale in the Urban Design of Montreal Residential Developments." M.Arch thesis. Montreal: McGill University, 1995.

Pollowy, Anne Marie. *The Urban Nest*. Stroudsberg, PA: Dowolen, Hutchinson & Ross, Inc., 1977.

Rybczynski, Witold. "The New Downtowns," *Atlantic Monthly* (May 1993): 98–102.

Winnipeg, City of. "Neighbourhood Designation Report (March 2000)." Winnipeg: Community Services Department, 2000.

## Chapter 7: Home as a Consumer Product

Blakely, Edward J., and Mary Gail Snyder. "Forting Up: Gated Communities in the United States," *Journal of Architectural and Planning Research* 15, 1 (Spring 1998): 61–72.

– *Fortress America: Gated Communities in the United States*. Washington, DC: Brookings Institution Press, 1997.

Cornwall, Thomas. "Successful Houses. VIII," *The House Beautiful* 2, 6 (November 1897): 137–42.

Dent, Laura E. "A Study of Design Codes with Specific Reference to Contemporary Suburban Housing." M.Arch. thesis. Montreal: McGill University, 1993.

Forty, Adrian. *Objects of Desire*. New York: Pantheon Books Inc., 1993.

Garigliano, Jeff. "Shelter Titles Square Off," *Folio: The Magazine for Magazine Management* (1 February 1997): 17–18.

Garreau, Joel. *Edge City: Life on the New Frontier*. New York: Doubleday, 1991.

Lane, Robert. "Successful Houses. VII," *The House Beautiful* 2, 6 (November 1897): 122–8.

Langdon, Philip. "Dissecting the American House," *Progressive Architecture* (October 1995): 45–51.

– *A Better Place to Live: Reshaping the American Suburb*. Amherst: University of Massachusetts, 1994.

– "Housing an Aging Nation," *Atlantic Monthly* (April 1988): 67–9.

– "A Good Place to Live," *Atlantic Monthly* (March 1988): 39–60.

– "The American House," *Atlantic Monthly* (September 1984): 45–73.

Polonsky, Michael Jay, and Alma Mintu-Wimsatt eds., *Environmental Marketing*. New York: The Haworth Press, 1995.

Schoenauer, Norbert. *6,000 Years of Housing*. New York: W.W. Norton, 2000.

– *Cities, Suburbs, Dwellings in the Postwar Era*. Montreal: McGill University School of Architecture, 1994.

Steffel, Jennifer. "Storming the Suburban Fortress: Understanding the NIMBY Phenomenon." M. Arch. thesis. Montreal: McGill University, 1996.

# Index